THE
Tree of Lives

A Journey Through Genealogy

by Joel Levitt

The Tree of Lives
A Journey Through Genealogy

by **Joel Levitt**

Published by

ARKETT PUBLISHING
division of Arkettype
PO Box 36, Gaylordsville, CT 06755
806-350-4007 • Fax 860-355-3970
www.arkett.com

ISBN 978-1-7950558-3-3

Printed in USA.

Dedication

For my grandparents,
who showed the courage to come to America.
Tillie Musicant Kaplan and Isaac Kaplan
Sarah Czenzov Levitt and Jacob Levitt

*"There is nothing new in the world
except the history you do not know."*
Harry Truman, President

*"I've been given all I wanted
Only three generations off the boat
I have harvested and I have planted
I am wearing my father's old coat."*
Paul Simon, Singer, Songwriter

Front Cover Concept: Barbara Levitt
Front Cover Photographs: Joel Levitt
Front Cover Design: Lou Okell

THE TREE OF LIVES

Introduction

On a brisk winter's day in 2016, my wife Barbara and I toured the Tenement Museum on the Lower East Side of Manhattan; a neighborhood that was the first stop for so many immigrants after leaving Ellis Island. There, a remarkable coincidence occurred, perhaps more suitable for a science fiction time traveler than a visitor from Connecticut.

The museum tells the true stories of real-life immigrant families from various cultures, all of whom at one time lived in this building over a 75-year period.

We stepped back in time to 1916, exactly 100 years earlier and into a tiny three-room apartment to meet a 14-year old girl named Victoria Confino, who lived there with nine other members of her extended family. Toilets were in the hall and shared with other families. Baths occurred only weekly at a nearby bath house. The rooms were authentically furnished for that period and a young, costumed actress told Victoria's story in the first person, never breaking character.

Her Sephardic Jewish family had escaped from war-torn Greece during the Ottoman era. They traveled to America as most immigrants did, including my grandparents, in steerage; the cheapest, most crowded and most unsanitary part of the boat. She was a factory worker at fourteen, with little formal education, but related an aspirational tale of immigrant life shared by many of the 7,000 inhabitants from 20 countries who had once lived at 97 Orchard St.

After we left the apartment, our guide explained to our tour group that the adult Victoria Confino had married a man named Cohen, moved to Brooklyn, was widowed and lived with her daughter Celia and her husband until her death at age 87. Her granddaughter Vicky, the guide continued, had worked with the museum to develop the program we had just seen. It wasn't until our trip home that I connected all the dots to come to an amazing conclusion.

I knew Victoria Confino.

I knew her 50 years later and only as Mrs. Cohen. She was the Sephardic immigrant mother of my parents' friends Celia and Stanley (with whom she lived), who had daughters named Vicky and Denise. I recalled hearing that after her grandmother died, Vicky volunteered at the museum. At the time, I did not know in what capacity (later confirmed by the family). What a loving tribute to a wonderful woman and to all immigrants from all nations.

From left, standing: Anna Levitt, Victoria Confino (Mrs. Cohen), daughter Celia Grubman   Seated: Lia Levitt, Joel Levitt, Son-in-law Stanley Grubman, 1980

This too, is a loving tribute, although I did not personally know many of my ancestors. It is however, their story and I have tried to craft it with love, understanding, honesty and respect.

Someday my descendants may read it and I want them to understand the courage it took for my maternal grandparents Tillie and Isaac Kaplan and paternal grandparents Sarah and Jacob Levitt to leave their roots and their families behind and make the precarious journey to America, the "Goldene Medina": the Golden Land. This is their tale, and in many ways the tale of all immigrants, spun with a golden thread.

Joel Levitt
Fall 2018

Part I: Roots

Families are filled with memories. They are memories not to be forgotten, but never to be replicated.

—Joel Levitt

Anna Kaplan, 1913

I remember many things about Brooklyn when I was growing up in the 1950s. Appliance store windows were filled with a newly popular invention called television, and folks who didn't own one yet (and most didn't) stared at them through the store windows.

Note that the ad encourages folks to watch the game at the store, since so few families had TVs.

We had one phone for the household and it was a "party line" shared with other families. Sometime you'd pick up the phone to make a call and there were already strangers on it having their own conversation. On sweltering summer days (no air conditioning, yet) there were regular visits from an organ grinder with accompanying monkey; watermelon was sold from the back of a truck; stickball was played in the streets, using a broom handle for a bat.

At supper time, mothers of varying ethnicities opened their apartment windows and shouted, "Suppah! Don't make me send your father out to get ya"; massive blocks of ice were delivered with giant tongs; sawdust covered the worn floors of butcher shops to catch the spilled blood; coal for furnaces slid down chutes into basement boiler rooms; penny candies actually cost a penny.

Our local Boro Park neighborhood bakery's rye bread was studded with caraway seeds, each warm loaf plastered with the bakery workers' union label. And they had a hard crust. I've never encountered a rye bread since, with a truly hard crust. We can clone a sheep. Why can't we clone a crust?

But my main memories are of my mother Anna, my father Louis, my brother Ira, my grandmothers Tillie and Sarah and the multitude of aunts, uncles, cousins and friends who populated my life and now, my memories.

How we got to America in the first place, is a story of courage: the courage to begin a new life in a new land.

My mother Anna Levitt, was the first and only one of her seven siblings to be born in America, in 1913. Her parents, Tillie Musicant and Isaac Kaplan both had been widowed, the former in Russia and the latter in America and Anna was their only child together; a generation younger than her siblings. Each had prior children. Tillie was the mother of Moses (later adopted by Isaac) and Isaac, the father of Israel, Fannie, Julius, Samuel, Joseph and Benjamin, later known as Morris.

I realize today, how fortunate I was in the early 1990s to have thought to interview my mother (then in her eighties) and collect notes about her early years and those of her family. My grandmother Tillie had saved a number of early photos and documents, both from here and Europe and my mother added many of her own over the years. Almost all of these my mother was able to identify and I wrote down the information on the backs of the photos. I wasn't particularly interested in genealogy at the time, but thought it was important to know for future reference.

My father Louis Levitt was also the first in his family born in America, in 1911, but several siblings preceded and followed him. His parents, Sarah Czenzov (Shenzov) and Jacob Levitt also had emigrated from within the "Pale of Settlement," the area of Eastern Europe where Jews were forced to live, often in poor communities called "shtetls." Their children were older sister and brother Anna (known as Elinor throughout adulthood) and Alex (Al) and younger sister and brother Sadie (known as Shirley) and Hyman (Hy). Another brother had died a few days after birth and before his bris (circumcision) and so by Jewish custom at the time, was unnamed.

Virtually all of the photos and documents of the Levitt family's early years were fortunately saved by my Aunt Elinor. They were recently discovered by my brother Ira in a box in his basement, years after he had served as co-executor of Elinor and her husband Isadore's estate.

Pale of Settlement. Note Kiev/Tarashcha in center (Muzykant),
Grodno in northwest (Kaplan), Vitebsk in northeast (Levitt),
Courtesy of Berdichev.org.

The Muzykants

The Muzykant family was from Tarashcha (Taraszcza) a small town near the capital Kiev, in central Ukraine. As the name implies, many of the male family members were musicians. Jews in Russia were forced to acquire surnames by the mid-19th century, in part for reasons of easier taxation and drafting availability into the Czar's army. The Russian czars were absolute rulers, who largely kept the Russian people as serfs, a form of economic servitude. Many Jews took names associated with their livelihood (Sandler: shoemaker, Einstein: mason, Portnoy: tailor, etc.).

Rafael HaLevy Muzykant (Philip Morrison), ca. 1900.

"Musicant" is a generic name for musician and pops up in literature and folklore. The Polish Nobel laureate (1905) Henryk Sienkiewicz's most famous novella is "Janko Muzykant (Johnny the Musician)," who is a peasant boy whose desire to play the fiddle brings him to a tragic end. There is also a statue dedicated to "Janko Muzykant" in the Polish town of Torun that commemorates the folk story of a young boy who rids his town of pesky frogs by playing his fiddle to lure them into the forest. Kind of like the Pied Piper of Poland.

The Jewish performers known as "Klezmer," a permitted occupation for Jews, were largely travelling musicians, central to the success of major life events such as weddings. Life was harsh, and weddings were a welcome cause for celebration for the entire community. Their tunes, led by the violinist, were both joyful and poignant and their occupations were often passed down from generation to generation of males, as we'll soon see in the lineage of the Philadelphia Muzykants (Morrisons).

Life in the shtetl of Tarashcha where the Jews lived, must have been anything but a wedding march, but I have no firsthand information. Tillie probably was reticent about it with Anna. Too many bad memories and my mother never really told me what, if anything, she knew about her mother's days in Ukraine. That was very common among the immigrant generation. Life had been hard and few wanted to transplant those harsh memories to America.

Barbara Siegel Lang, a fellow member of the "Tracing the Tribe" Facebook genealogy site contacted me to share some of the background about Tarashcha that her late father had told her. She wrote:

"My dad lived in Tarashcha till the age of 13. He had his Bar Mitzvah at the synagogue in Tarashcha and then along with his mother and younger brother joined his dad who had come to America 10 years before. They had no contact with him all those years. He (her father) came to the US in 1923. I heard some stories of the soldiers occupying their home, killing the family dog and increased attacks on the Jews, but mostly my dad told me funny stories. Now I believe he didn't want me to know. The rest of his family were killed."

And to a large extent, this is why I would say, most American Jews of my generation know so little about our immigrant ancestors' lives in "The Old County."

Jews had a long history in Tarashcha that ended tragically.

Tarashcha market square with roof of main synagogue in distance, ca. 1910

In the early 19th century the number of Jews living in the shtetl was over 5000, nearly fifty percent of the total population. The Jewish community suffered several pogroms (mob attacks) from local peasants during the Russian Revolutionary period of 1917-1920. Horrible times that were going to get worse.

In 1941 Nazi troops entered and took control of the approximately 500–600 Jews left, who now had to wear armbands with a yellow Star of David. Several mass executions ensued and it is estimated that 400–500 Jews of all ages were killed and buried in mass graves. It was a horrific scene repeated throughout Central and Eastern Europe.

The Voyage to America

Thanks to a cousin, Jeffrey Blustein who has done an amazing job of genealogical sleuthing, we can trace Tillie and Anna's family in Tarashcha back to Rafael "Folik" HaLevy Muzykant, who died before 1860. His son, Leib Baer Muzykant (born before 1840, died before 1906) was married to a woman named Hanah (no further information). They had six children: Rafael HaLevy (Philip), born ca.1865 in Tarashcha, died before 1942 in Philadelphia; Moshe (Morris), born ca.1870 in Tarashcha, died 1943 in Philadelphia; my grandmother Taube (Tillie), born about 1874 in Tarashcha, died 1956 in Brooklyn; Liba (Lena), born around 1868 in Tarashcha, died in New York City around 1954; and Chava, who was born and died in Tarashcha and who, by my estimation was born ca. 1860 and died after 1937.

Rafael HaLevy, the oldest son, undoubtedly made the initial decision to come to America.

The emotional dislocation of leaving the Old Country for the New must have been staggering, in spite of the horrors of the Old. For most, the voyage to America was harrowing and the sheer number of immigrants, beyond comprehension. In 1907 alone, 1,285,349 immigrants arrived in America. Poor people made the voyage in "steerage," the darkest, dirtiest, deepest deck of vessels that held up to 3000 people. The trip took between one and two weeks.

According to Musicant family lore both in Brooklyn and Philadelphia, Tillie's oldest brother Rafael HaLevy emigrated to America first, settled in Philadelphia, then sent for his wife Fannie (Faigel) and children when he was financially able to support them. He later sent for his younger brother and two of his sisters, including Tillie in whatever order, we do not know. All of that seems plausible, but inadvertently, untrue.

According to the "List of Manifest of Alien Passengers for the U.S. Immigration Officer at Port of Arrival" (www.ancestry. com), the SS Vaderland departed from Antwerp, Belgium on March, 24, 1906 and arrived in NYC on April 3, 1906.

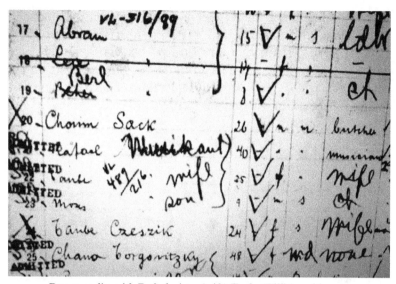

Passenger list with Rafael, sister (wife) Taube (Tillie) and her son Moses Musikant, 1906

The Vaderland had an interesting history. It was launched in 1900 for the Red Star Line as a passenger ship. At the outbreak of World War 1, it was converted to a troop ship and in 1915 was renamed the Southland (Vaderland sounding too Germanic). It was torpedoed twice during the war; the second time by a German submarine, sinking in 1917. All but four of the troops aboard were saved.

SS Vaderland

15

Among its passengers in 1906 and stamped as "Admitted" were Rafael "Musikant" (later Philip Morrison), age 40, a musician and "Hebrew" from "Tarasz," his "wife" Taube (later Tillie Musicant), age 25 and a child named Moses (later Morris Musicant), age 9. They were to join relatives already here: an uncle, D. Formann in New York and brother (unnamed, of the uncle). They actually lived at 335 St. Ann's Ave., near 142 St. in the Bronx.

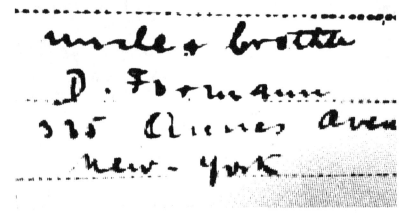

The 1906 ship manifest states that the "Musikants" will be staying with D. Formann, uncle and his brother.

Anna had said that Tillie initially lived in the Bronx immediately after arriving in New York. The uncle's surname listed on the ship's manifest was Formann, but spellings in those days varied and a Formann could not be found in the early censuses. There is, however, a tailor named Davis Foreman listed in the 1905 NYS Census, b. ca. 1861, living in the Bronx with wife Anna and children, one of whom is a fifteen-year old, named David, the youngest and only one of the children born in the United States.

Davis Foreman was a match. The uncle had been found!

Growing up, I had never heard of a relative named Foreman, but apparently, Tillie and Anna had kept in touch with the Foreman family, at least until the early years of my parents' marriage.

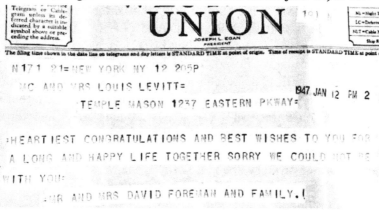

	Carolina	Daughter	W	F	5	United States
England—Emanuel		Lodger	W	F	46	Germany
	Frank	Lodger	W	m	16	United States
Nusbaum—Frank		Head	W	m	77	United States
	Anna	Wife	W	F	76	United States
	Adrian	Son	W	m	1	United States
Conary—Bryan		Head	W	m	54	Ireland
	Hannah	Wife	W	F	19	United States
Foreman—Davis		Head	W	m	44	Russia
	Anna	Wife	W	F	42	Austria

Davis Foreman and his wife, Anna are listed in the bottom row of the 1905 NYS Census. He was 44 years old at the time and from Russia, and she was age 42 and from Austria. They were Tillie and Rafael's aunt and uncle.

A Western Union telegram from the Manhattan office was sent to Anna and Louis from "David Foreman and Family," the son of Davis. He tells them that he is sorry he cannot make their wedding and wishes them well. It's dated Jan. 12, 1947.

Western Union telegram from David Foreman and Family, 1/12/47

In the 1940 US census, David Foreman (b. 7/18/90) is listed as the manager of a real estate office. His wife's name is Sarah and they have two daughters; Anna (most likely named after his late mother), age 21 and Yvette, age 14. They are renters and all of them had been born in NYC. They must have been well off, because living with them was a cousin, Pearl Elbert and a servant, Beatrice Partlo.

1940 US Census lists David and Sarah Foreman and Family

To complicate things somewhat, as a last-ditch effort to decipher the address of the original Formanns, I posted a photo of it on a Facebook Jewish genealogy site that drew an astonishing response. While I had never heard of the name Foreman before, another relatively unknown name popped up. A respondent replied that she had been doing research on an unrelated family and found that same name and address in the Bronx as the destination of one Meier Bariskin. Bariskin travelled on that same ship and on that same voyage to that same uncle at that same location. And like Rafael, Meier was a musician from Taraschcha! His birth year is given as 1879. Bariskin sounded familiar to me and I recalled that it must be another spelling of Baretskin, the name listed on Tillie and Isaac's 1908 marriage certificate in the Bronx, as her father's name ("Laeb Baretskin") and as her name ("Tillie Baretskin Musicant"), although in actuality, those relationships appear to be a clerical error. Tillie's father was Leib Baer Muzykant. So now, another mystery opened. Perhaps the Muzykants traveled to America with a cousin, Meier Bariskin.

Meier Bariskin arrived as many others, while his wife Schifre Baraskin (surname spelled differently on her ship manifest), whose maiden name was Bloom, and two children, Isidor and Frank remained in Russia. She and the children arrived three months later on the SS Mississippi. By the 1910 US Census, he had become Meyer Boriskin and his wife, Sophie and they now had five children (Isidor, 10; Frank, 5; Fannie, 3; Annie, 2; and newborn Levi). Meyer was listed as having his own band. Brother Harry was born in 1913 and sister Sarah in 1920. Tragically, that same year, Fannie died in the Great Influenza Epidemic of 1920. Meyer died at age 71 in 1950.

I recently located Meyer Boriskin's great-grandson Michael Kosarin, an Emmy award winning and Grammy award nominated music director, conductor, arranger and composer. We exchanged emails without making definitive family connections. Since Michael's DNA tests and my own were from different companies, our results could not be compared. Michael then found a site called DNALand, where incompatible DNA results could be uploaded to see if they matched. Ours did not.

I also recently found Levi (Louis) Boriskin's son Michael, who is a noted concert pianist and Aaron Copland scholar and who was amazed at the possibility of a Boriskin/ Muzykant connection. It is possible that further DNA testing might yield a genetic match, but right now there is only circumstantial evidence and of course, the shared love of music.

So, who was Meier Boriskin and why was he traveling on the same ship from the same town with the same occupation to the same uncle, yet somehow, not a blood relative? One theory I have is that "D. Formann" may have served as a kind of "good uncle" to immigrants from his hometown of Tarashcha, who needed an official sponsor already living in America. It remains a tantalizing genealogical mystery.

We also know from Tillie's 1908 marriage certificate, that her mother is listed as, "Manie Forman," so Davis Formann was a maternal uncle. The name Formann, is also occupational in origin. It refers to a carter, or one who drives a horse-drawn wagon filled with goods.

Taube (in Yiddish) was my grandmother Tillie and why she was listed as Rafael's wife, instead of as his sister is open to interpretation. The simplest is that the Antwerp clerk who took down the information got it wrong (since the Muzykants only spoke Yiddish), like so many other census takers and official scribes.

Another possible explanation is that Rafael was trying to protect his sister aboard ship; a 25-year old widow with a young child, from single men with potentially bad intentions. Men and women (even if married) slept in different areas of the ship. This is a reverse of what the Hebrew Bible (Genesis12:5) describes the patriarch Abraham as doing:

"There was a famine in the land. Abram (later Abraham) headed south to Egypt to stay there for a while, since the famine had grown very severe in the land. As they approached Egypt, he said to his wife Sarai (later Sarah), 'I realize that you are a good-looking woman. When the Egyptians see you, they will assume that you are my wife and kill me, allowing you to live. If you would, say that you are my sister. They will then be good to me for your sake, and through your efforts, my life will be spared.'"

Abraham apparently devised that ruse to save his own "tuchis," but I believe Rafael as an older brother reversed the relationships by claiming Tillie (Taube) was his wife, saving his sister from harassment, or worse. Who knows? But I'm going with the noble explanation.

In the early 21st century his grandson Herman Morrison, then in his eighties, published his memoir, a warm remembrance of his mother's and father's families, graciously sent to me by his daughter, Denise Stredler. He described how Muzykant became Morrison at Ellis Island, as told to him by his father, Jacob.

Sarah and Jacob Morrison (Herman's parents). Jacob was a musician and owned a barber shop in Philadelphia. Herman Morrison, 1918-2007

"When my Zayde (grandfather) first came to Ellis Island, the U.S. Custom guards asked him his name. He had no identification. They couldn't understand what he was telling them, but did understand the first letter of his name, which sounded like an "M." They wrote down Morrison, gave him his required and necessary identification, pointed to an official card that said Morrison and passed him through the gate."

While that's an oft-told tale of immigration, it appears that it is not necessarily historically accurate. Stories of immigration officers changing names are historically not true, according to experts in the field. It appears that historians agree that they wrote down the names that appeared on the ship's manifest and in this case was spelled at point of departure as, "Musikant." Also, if his brother Moishe (Morris) Muzykant arrived in 1910, his name certainly could not have been coincidentally changed at Ellis Island to Morrison. Rafael's sister Taube, who came on the same ship, was never a Morrison and remained a Muzykant (spelled Musicant) until she remarried. It appears probable that Rafael changed his name to Philip Morrison and when Moshe arrived in Philadelphia, he followed suit to become Morris Morrison. Still, Herman's narrative makes a great story and I appreciate his retelling of it.

The Morrison Brothers

Rafael HaLevy Muzykant of Tarashcha became Philip Morrison of Philadelphia. He eventually brought not only his wife Fannie and their five children to America, but also his younger brother Moshe, who became Morris Morrison and his wife Fannie, by 1910. He also arranged for the arrival of his younger sister, the widowed Liba Monastersky, who became Lena.

Why Philadelphia is anyone's guess, but (and this is pure conjecture) it is possible that they were influenced the great Yiddish theatre actor and impresario Boris Thomashefsky and his actress wife, Bessie (both from the Tarashcha area). In 1889 they founded the first Yiddish theatre in Philadelphia (the Thomashefskys were the grandparents of the famous American conductor, Michael Tilson Thomas). Their stay in Philly was brief, but it may have created a connection for Tillie's older brother Rafael HaLevy Muzykant.

Boris and Bessie Thomashefsky, ca. 1890
Thomashefsky Foundation

From left: Rafael Morrison and wife Fannie, standing;
Morris Morrison and wife Fannie, standing, ca.1910, Philadelphia

Philip and Morris Morrison re-established their musical credentials in Philadelphia. Herman Morrison recalled:

"Zayda (his grandfather Philip) played the violin with his own orchestra called the Philip Morrison Orchestra, at parties, weddings, Bar Mitzvahs, and ballroom dances. His clarinet player was my father (Jacob Morrison) who used to practice upstairs at our home. Zayda was the first person ever to publish a song sheet that had all of the popular songs of the day and distributed them everywhere his orchestra played and got all the people to join his sing-a-long....He composed music for all the instruments in his orchestra, hand-written music but didn't know how to present the music (copyright/publish) or to whom."

Left Photo: Fannie and Philip Morrison.
Right Photo: Fannie and Morris Morrison, ca. early 1940s

Anna remembered her Philadelphia relatives fondly. In the 1920's Anna and her parents Tillie and Isaac Kaplan used to travel from NYC to Philly by train. They sometimes stayed with Philip's family and sometimes with Morris's. The brothers had purchased homes very close to each other in South Philadelphia, a poor and working-class neighborhood. "Each," Anna recalled, "owned their own small two-story brick home with marble steps on narrow cobblestone streets." Anna used to love visiting her Philly family, "because they were so nice to us." When the Kaplans visited the Morrisons, they all would go on a picnic. "I think," Anna said, "they even brought their instruments."

Above left: Tillie's Philly niece (daughter of older brother Philip Morrison) and nephew-to-be; Fannie Morrison and fiancé Sam Dubinsky (Dubin), ca. 1915. Yiddish inscription on back reads, "Dear aunt and uncle Toibe and Mr. Kaplan (it was a second marriage, so Isaac Kaplan was addressed more formally) I, Fannie and my fiancé Sam wish you a happy, healthy year and may we soon see each other at my wedding. From your niece Fannie and your future nephew Sam Dubinsky."

Above right: Family picnic with Jacob Morrison, Fannie Morrison Dubin and Sam Dubin, standing; Philip Morrison, Isaac Kaplan seated; Jack Dubin on ground.

Sam Dubin in his snazzy, jazzy car. All photos except engagement photo, dated June 17, 1923 in Philadelphia area

Philly Fashionistas: Left: Tillie's niece Becky Morrison, daughter of brother
Philip Morrison and second wife, also named Fannie. Photo dated June 13, 1923.
Right: Tillie's grandniece (unidentified),
granddaughter of brother Morris Morrison, ca. 1920s.

Tillie's grandniece (unidentified), ca. 1920s

In the next generation, Lou Morrison (1908-1990), one of Anna's cousins and son of Morris was a well-known Philadelphia area pianist, performing in bands throughout the region. He was remembered by one of his granddaughters as having performed with renowned band leader Guy Lombardo (of New Year's Eve fame), and was always in demand as a "session" player. The July 2, 1949 edition of "Billboard" magazine announced, "Lou Morrison, who led the band at the Embassy Club (Philadelphia) all year will play the piano 'lulls' over the summer season." Among many other Lou Morrison venues, were the Anchorage Inn and the Swan Club. Lou was so highly regarded locally that "Billboard" (October 23, 1943) heralded his being, "...grabbed up by WIBG for a series of solo piano rambling sessions."

Philadelphia's WIBG was a unique radio station. It originally began in 1925 as a Christian broadcaster; its initials standing for "Why I Believe in God." After it was sold, it morphed into a Big Band station in the 1940s and early '50s, changing again a few years later to feature one of the first all "Rock N Roll" formats in the USA.

Tillie's nephew Lou Morrison, ca. 1930s

Philadelphia itself, has an interesting Jewish musical history. In "American Klezmer. It's Roots and Offshoots" (University of California Press, 2002), editor Mark Slobin referred to a Philadelphia musician; "A klezmer named Mr. Morrison was well known, both for his ability to play many instruments and his refusal to distinguish one from the other." I believe he was referring to my great-uncle Philip.

"Most of the clubs (including the Embassy, where Lou Morrison reigned) that used to dominate Philadelphia's live entertainment scene," according to a 2003 article in "Philadelphia Jewish Life" by Murray Friedman, "were Jewish owned or operated, some having evolved from Prohibition-era speakeasies."

Left photo: Millie (1906-1976) and Louis Morrison (1908-1990). Photo inscribed: "Presented by Mr. and Mrs. Louis Morrison to his Aunt and Uncle Kaplan (Tillie and Isaac Kaplan), Nov. 1 1939.

Liba Muzykant

Liba Muzykant Monastersky
April, ca. 1942. Photo courtesy of
Stacy Silverstein Simon

I knew nothing about Tillie, Philip and Morris's sister Liba (Lena) until I saw her name in Jeff Blustein's extensive Muzykant family tree. I don't recall Anna ever mentioning her and her photo was not among those of the Philadelphia Morrisons Tillie had saved. I didn't know why Liba seemed to have become the "forgotten" Muzykant sibling.

I had been reluctant to undergo the simple DNA testing, because I already knew where my ancestry evolved from and had heard of tales of multitudes of "cousins" discovered through the test who apparently shared DNA, but had no known family connections. Nearing the end of this two-year project, I did not want to complicate its completion chasing hundreds of potential distant relatives. It was complicated enough chasing down the relatives I knew about. Boy, was I wrong.

Yes, the test did tell me what I had suspected. I am 95 percent Eastern European Jewish, but it also furnished me with a list of 1000 plus folks who were DNA related. Starting with the "Extremely High" matches, I contacted 90 people and received about 35 replies, which I understand is an excellent response. One of those was from Merle Pullar of Virginia and we discovered that we are indeed related. Merle's mother was Daris Merlin Kanas; her grandmother was Minnie (Mitzi) Monastersky Merlin Feldman and her great-grandmother was Liba Muzykant Monastersky April, my grandmother Tillie's sister. Missing no more!

Merle put me in touch with her cousin (and now mine) Jeffrey Rappoport, a retired Staten Island rabbi, who now lives in Jerusalem. Jeffrey is a natural-born storyteller and a repository of much family lore about his great-grandmother Liba and her daughter Mitzi, who both lived with Jeffrey's family when he was growing up. I'll let him tell their story:

"Bubba Liba was married to Jack April (her second husband). He was a gentleman farmer. He grew mostly apples, but he also raised cattle. I have very vague memories of being on his farm (in Southeast CT). He also had a shul on his farm where men came to pray for Shabbat. Bubba Liba lived with my original parents at the end of her life. We lived on 65th Ave. (in Queens). She died in that house. I do not know where Marvin was that day, but Harold and I were out on his pretzel truck and came home to find her dead.... "

"Bubba Liba did not speak any English. I used to scream at her in Yiddish (translation), You are a 'greener'. Stop speaking mamaloshen and speak English. This is America'. The only words she knew in English were curse words. She would shout, 'Goddam it. Shit, shit. Goddam it. Shit, shit', Always like that. She would hit us with her cane. She also was a mean pincher. She would grab, pinch and twist. I guess she was ahead of her time. She created the purple murple...."

"Bubba Liba was short-under five feet tall. Then again, so was Bubby Mitzi. Actually, you knew that Bubba Liba was Bubby Mitzi's mother the minute you looked at her. Same face. Same build. Same nose."

"Bubba Liba was stocky and busty. She wore shoes with buttons. As I wrote, she swung a mean cane. She believed that every meal had to start with soup. When I would yell at her to speak English, she would encourage me by saying, 'Ess soop'. Or it could have been ess up. I was never quite sure. She thought she was speaking English. She wore thick glasses and had a very stern visage. She was blessed with Russian legs and 'kankles'. She wore her hair up. She loved to render chicken fat (schmaltz). Every Sunday, she would stand in the kitchen with the hock messer and chopping bowl and make chopped liver. At dinner, we would spread the schmaltz on rye bread and eat it with the liver. She did make a mean chopped liver. It was one of my favorites. After dinner, she would go up to her room, not to be seen until the next day. She would listen to the Yiddish radio shows all day long...."

"Bubba Liba had a special talent... When couples got married, for a gift she gave them hand sewn tachrichim (burial shrouds). Seems a lot weird to me, but according to our mom, people appreciated them very much. She made them herself."

"Bubba Mitzi (Liba's daughter) was a card. She had a robust sense of humor. She also enjoyed 'dirty' jokes. She could tell some racy jokes, but when I was in college, and we would speak on the phone every week, she would say, 'Got a dirty joke for Bubby?' She was a natural storyteller. In her early years, she had been a wet nurse for babies whose mothers did not produce milk. In Russia, she had been a fortune teller. Once in America, she refused to do it. She said that now that she lived in America, she did not believe in it anymore...."

"She had one amazing talent. When women in the family were pregnant, she would rub their belly and then somberly announce whether it was a boy or a girl. She was NEVER wrong. When my wife was pregnant with our daughter Tali, Bubby did her prognostication over the phone. She got that one right, also...." (author's note: my mother Anna, Mitzi's cousin, used to do the same).

"When I was in the pulpit, my sermons often included stories of bubby and pappy. Soon the whole congregation grew to love her, even though they had never met. One year, mom and dad brought her to Rosh Hashana at our house on Staten Island. After Services, I would stand in the hall way and greet people as they left the shul. I announced that bubby would stand with me. She stood there for close to thirty minutes as people left. Over and over again, she would say, 'That's right. I'm the bubba. I made him a mensch.' What was interesting was that she was using a cane in those days, and yet she stood on her feet for so long to greet people..."

While Jeffrey supplied a string of colorful anecdotes, I still did not have the specifics of the branch of the Muzykant family tree descended from Liba. I decided to do some additional online research and found some information on the MyHeritage site ascribed to a Silverstein Family Tree managed by someone named Stacy Silverstein. I thought I might find Stacy on Facebook and among several with that name was the one I was hoping for. I messaged her and she immediately responded with, "Liba was my great-great-grandmother."

"Wow," I messaged back. Stacy was an amazing and generous resource. She emailed me what turned into an 18-page printout of Liba's branch of the family tree that she had originally started as a teenager. Finally, just a couple of months before going to print, I had an extensive list of virtually all of the American Muzykant siblings' descendants.

Stacy attached notes that indicated that Liba was a widow with four children when she emigrated to America in 1914, settling among her brothers' families in Philadelphia. In Ukraine, she had been a midwife. The father of her children had been Yosef Monastersky. One of Liba and Yosef's children, their oldest son Yaakov (Yasha) remained in Ukraine, but Anna (Nachomi), Minnie (Mitzi) and Morris (known as Muzzy) came with their mother.

Liba's second husband was Morris April, the gentleman farmer referred to in Jeffrey Rappoport's recollections. They did not have children together.

From Sidewalk Tap Dancer to the Metropolitan Opera Ballet

Zachary Solov in flight
Photo courtesy of Zachary Solov Foundation

As a child, Anna once told me that we had a cousin from Philadelphia named Zachary Solov, who was a dancer in a ballet company in the 1940s. "He was a slim fellow, not married," she said and marveled at, "how graceful he was when he got up (from a chair), like a dancer gets up." I don't recall her ever mentioning him again until her recollection of him when she was in her eighties.

Zachary Solov was more than a ballet dancer. He was, at his prime, the Ballet Master/Choreographer of the Metropolitan Opera Ballet in NYC and his death in 2004 merited an obituary in "The New York Times" and Broadway's

"Playbill." In 2011, the Zachary Solov Foundation donated his papers to the New York Public Library for the Performing Arts at Lincoln Center.

Joel Levitt and cousin Zachary Solov as young men. Any resemblance?
Photo at right courtesy of Zachary Solov Foundation

Born in Philadelphia in 1923 to two deaf parents, Zachary's biographer Dean Temple (as of 2018, the biography has not been completed) speculated in Zachary's obituary in the "New York Sun" that his parents' deafness had had a formative impact on his ability to communicate with his body.

Young Zachary was discovered tap dancing on the sidewalks of his neighborhood, which in turn led to his formal dance education. As a child, he danced with Charles "Honi" Coles (1911 or 12-1992), a trailblazing African American tap dance giant, also from Philly. In 1991, Coles was awarded the National Medal of the Arts.

As a child, Zachary also appeared on "The Horn and Hardart (of Automat fame) Children's Hour" radio program. Drafted into the Army during WW ll, he performed in and choreographed 35 army revues in the US and Asia. Zachary regularly staged dance routines at Radio City Music Hall for the Rockettes, partnered with Latin American music star Carmen Miranda at the famed Roxy Theatre, performed with dance pioneer George Balanchine's American Ballet and appeared on Broadway as a dancer with star Jackie Gleason and on early television show such as, "Omnibus," and Sid Caesar's "Your Show of Shows."

Zachary Solov and Janet Collins, 1951
Photo courtesy of Zachary Solov Foundation

One of Zachary's most notable achievements was his hiring of Janet Collins as the first African-American principal dancer at the Metropolitan Opera, four years before the great American contralto Marian Anderson (and Danbury, CT resident) broke the operatic color barrier at the Met (who was awarded both a National Medal of the Arts and a Presidential Medal of

Freedom). Zachary was only 28 years old when he was appointed Ballet Master, but he moved very quickly to bring Ms. Collins on stage. As described in Zachary's "Los Angeles Times" obituary, "Collins arrived in 1949 (to NYC) and earned glowing reviews in a variety of performances, including Cole Porter's musical, 'Out of this World'. It was in that role that she was noticed by Zachary Solov, then the ballet master of the Met."

"'She walked across the stage pulling a chiffon curtain and it was electric,' Solov recalled years later, 'The body just spoke.'"

Carmen de Lavallade, dancer, actress and choreographer and recent (2017) Kennedy Center honoree was Ms. Collins's cousin. She was quoted as saying, "I just want to thank Zachary for being such a courageous person in a time of history when people of color were not recognized for their worth. And that he hired Janet Collins to be the Prima Ballerina of the Met Opera."

When my mother had observed that Zachary was, "not married," she did not realize in those days that he was a gay man. Zachary's longtime partner was "The New York Times" dance critic John Martin. They shared an apartment on W. 58 St. in Manhattan and a house in Saratoga Springs, NY, home of the National Museum of Dance.

I regret that I came to genealogy so late in life that I never had the opportunity to meet this amazing man.

Tillie Musicant's Story

Tillie Musicant Kaplan having fun, ca. 1948

My maternal grandmother was known by four names during her lifetime: Tova (Hebrew), Taube (Yiddish), Tanya (Russian) and Tillie (English). She was born in 1874 or 1875 or 1878 or 1879 according to various censuses and forms, in Tarashcha, Ukraine, then part of Czarist Russia. Little is clear of her early life, although she was married there to a man named Yehudah Lib HaKohane, who had died sometime before 1906, when she left Russia. They had a son named Moshe (Moses), born ca.1895 who emigrated with her. Her 1908 NYC Marriage Records certificate does little to clarify the story. On the form (available at www.familysearch.com), she is referred to as "Tillie Baretskin Musicant," her father as "Laebe Baretskin." and her mother as Manie Forman."

It would imply that Tillie's maiden name was Baretskin, yet all other research indicates that she was born a Muzykant, as described on the 1906 ship manifest and throughout her life.

In her US Certificate of Naturalization, dated Feb. 25, 1944, Tillie is listed as age 63, married at age 30, now with gray hair and gray eyes, at five feet one inch tall and weighing 148 pounds. It all points out the difficulties of obtaining accurate information when folks spoke only Yiddish (or a multitude of other languages) and census and other recorders, while literate, were not necessarily well educated.

Tillie Kaplan Naturalization Document, 1944

We know that Tillie had brothers Philip (Rafael HaLevy) and Morris (Moshe) and a sister Lena (Liba) who lived in Philadelphia. A photo postcard sent from Tarashcha in 1908 to Tillie from brother Morris indicates that he and his fiancee Fanny emigrated in 1910, soon after their marriage, probably heading straight to Philadelphia after Ellis Island. Another sister Chava (Russian name, Klara) remained in Russia. Her birth date is unknown, but possibly ca. 1860 and date of death is unknown, but based on dated photos, was after 1937. Only Chava (married name, Noskin, also translated as Vaskins, but most agree with the former), and her husband Avram did not emigrate. Why?

Presumably, she was the oldest sibling, or at least, sister and she might not have left because of her family. Perhaps her husband Avram did not want to emigrate.

Photos dated 1925 and 1937 sent from Russia and saved by Tillie and Anna have inscriptions on the backs in Russian and/or Yiddish, neither of which I can read. My mother, when I reviewed them with her (then in her eighties, mentally sharp, but legally blind) peered at the photos at close range that she hadn't seen in decades and identified an elderly woman as Tillie's older sister, although she did not recall her name. Utilizing a couple of Facebook genealogy pages ("Tracing the Tribe" and "Jewish Genealogy Portal"), I posted the inscriptions, seeking translations. Several people were kind enough to respond and really helped clarify some of the uncertainty surrounding the photos.

Above left: Tillie's older sister Chava Noskin. Right: Chava's daughter Sanya on left and Sanya's oldest daughter Manya on right. Photos dated 1925

Inscriptions on backs of above photos. Curiously, the postcards are printed in English and French and neither contains postage. The upper card (photo above left) translates as, "For my dear sister Taube (Tillie's Yiddish name) with her family." Lower card (photo above right) translates as, "For memory of dear Aunt Tanya (Tillie's Russian name) with her family, from her niece Sanya with daughter Manya." Sanya and Manya are Russian names. Dated 1925

Tillie"s sister Chava and family, Tarashcha.

Remaining family in Tarashcha. Chava seated at center. Note military uniforms.

Above Left: Tillie's sister Chava in center, daughters and grandson, Nyuma (Benjamin) 1937. Above Right: Chava Noskin, 1937

Top inscription (corresponds to top photo of Chava and relatives): Translated as, "For eternal memory for Uncle Moisey (Moshe) and Aunt Fanya (Fannie), (from) Chava, Tzira, Sima, Nyuma (Nyuma is a secular name for Veniamin, or Benjamin in English)." 2/15/37. Bottom inscription (corresponds to top photo of Chava, alone): Translated as, "For good memory to my dear brother Moisey from sister Chava Noskin." Undated, but same as above.

Photo and back, inscribed (in same handwriting as notes at left, "To my dear brother Moisey, from Solomon, 2/19/38. Who Solomon was, is a mystery. It is possible that he is a cousin. One translator suggested that cousins often addressed each other in Russian, as, "brother." All of these inscriptions are written in what appears to be the same handwriting and in the same ink and at the same time (exact dates vary per translator). What military-like service or rank Solomon held is also undetermined.

41

Chava and Tillie's other relatives also appear in a poignant cemetery photo. My mother had told me that this undated photo had been taken at Tillie's parents' graves and sent to her mother, because the family that remained in Tarashcha knew that she would never come back. I cannot imagine the deep sadness of leaving your family and your ancestors, understanding that you would never return.

Photo at left: Tillie's parents' graves, Tarashcha. Tillie's niece Sanya kneeling at left. Tillie's sister Chava standing on right. Image at right: Etching I had done in college based on the photograph, 1968

Any surviving correspondence with Tillie's Tarashcha relatives ended in 1938 and for that matter, any surviving Levitt correspondence with relatives in Vitebsk ended in 1935. The situation in Eastern Europe was extremely tense in the late 1930s and early 1940s. Germany invaded the Soviet Union in 1941 and the results on the Eastern Front were devastating. Of the estimated 70 million deaths that occurred during World War ll, about 30 million were within the Eastern Front.

Left Photo: Tillie seated with unidentified cousin, standing. The Bronx, ca. 1907.
Right Photo: Tillie's son Moses (Morris) Musicant Kaplan with aunt, possibly
Morris Morrison's wife, Fannie., the Bronx, ca. 1910

Photo dated 1908 sent from Tarashcha by Tillie's brother Moshe and his fiancée Fannie, with inscription below.

It has been partially translated as saying that Moshe is very upset and heartbroken that Taube (Tillie) had not answered his correspondence. He has concluded that it is "bashert (fated)" that she will not be at
their wedding. That's interesting, since Tillie had emigrated only two years earlier and it would have been highly unrealistic to expect her to make that awful reverse trip to Ukraine, but families are complicated. Still, there were apparently no hard feelings, as Morris and Tillie visited each other when he emigrated and settled in Philadelphia. I could not discover who "Mr. H. Fotunick" was, although he might have been related to the Forman/Formann/Fortman family of Tillie's mother.

Photo left: Feigel (Fannie) fiancée, and later wife of Tillie's brother Morris (Moishe) Morrison (Muzykant). Sent from Tarashcha, 1/21/07. Photographed at P. Dzius Studio, Tarashcha, Ukraine. Photo right: Inscribed, "On the eternal and good memory to dear aunt Tanya (Tillie) from Versya (diminutive of Vera). Baby is unidentified. Photo taken at Visit Studio, Kiev, Ukraine, 1/1/08

Isaac Kaplan's Story

Isaac Kaplan, ca. 1920.

My grandfather Isaac Kaplan's story features little information about his early life, except for two documents that were fortunately and remarkably saved. One is the aforementioned marriage certificate and more importantly, the other is his naturalization paper.

The naturalization paper ("United States of America Declaration of Intention") dated Nov. 9, 1915 provides substantially more information. In it, Isaac is listed as 55 years old, born April 12, 1860, weighing 170 lbs. and at a height of five feet five inches with brown hair and gray eyes. He lived at 494 Levonia (Livonia) Ave. in Brooklyn at the time of the application.

Isaac states that he was born in Grodner (Grodno), Russia and his last foreign residence as Choinsk (Chomsk, Khomsk) in Russia. As required by the US, he renounces, "forever all allegiance and fidelity to any foreign prince, potentate, state or sovereignty, and particular to Nicholas ll, Emperor of All the Russias."

Isaac Kaplan Naturalization Document 1915

45

One of the difficulties of tracing one's roots to Eastern Europe is that the same city or town could be situated in one country one year and another in a different year, based on who had successfully invaded the region. Grodno, Isaac's birthplace was at various times part of Lithuania, Poland, Russia and today, Belarus.

The Jewish community of Grodno was well established by 1816, constituting over 85 percent of the town. By 1876 (about 20 years before Isaac emigrated), Grodno's Jewish population had peaked to over 27,000, although the percentage of the total population was down to about 68 percent. By that time Grodno had passed through Lithuanian hands, then Polish control and was by the early 19th century under Russian sovereignty.

Grodno's Jews worked primarily in agricultural commerce and as artisans. The city became a center for Talmudic learning and by 1793 a Jewish printing press opened in the town. In the 1890s Grodno became an active center for the Zionist movement, offering tangible support for those promoting Jewish settlement in Palestine.

Grodno's main synagogue

While many Jews appeared to have a more "cosmopolitan" life in Grodno, than in Tillie's hometown of Tarashcha, the community was not a stranger to anti-Semitism, which culminated in the tragedies during the Holocaust. The Germans occupied Grodno in 1941 and divided the Jewish population into two ghettos: one with 15,000 Jews deemed "Productive" and the other with 10,000 Jews labelled "Unproductive."

Most Jews were deported to concentration camps in Auschwitz and Treblinka. About 1000 were sent to the Bialystok ghetto. By the time the Russian Red Army entered the town in 1944, only about 250 Jews were alive.

Isaac emigrated (escaped his fate, more likely) in 1898. At that point he lived with his wife Dora (possibly named Vera, but likely, Dora) and family in Chomsk, a smaller community, but also in the Grodno district. My mother did not know whether he had siblings (probably, as families were larger then) or if his parents were alive at the time he left (he was about 38). She said he had been a bookbinder in the Old Country, but on his naturalization papers his employment is listed as tailor.

In discovering Isaac's naturalization paper, I discovered a surprise. Unlike the vast majority of European immigrants of all ethnicities during the 19th and early 20th centuries, Isaac did not come through Ellis Island. His ship, the "Canada" made port in Boston, sailing from Liverpool, England.

The SS Canada was built in Belfast and launched in 1896 under the Dominion Line. During the Boer War in South Africa (1899-1902) she served as a troop carrier, but generally took passengers to Canada in the summers and Boston in the winters. During World War l, she again carried troops and later served as an accommodation ship for German prisoners of war. She ceased service in 1926 and was scrapped in Italy.

The Canada had an investigatory connection to the sinking of the famed Titanic. At the 1912 official inquiry following the tragedy, R.O. Jones, the captain of the Canada testified that his ship had also received ice warning wireless (telegraph) messages while in the same ice field as the ill-fated ship. He testified that he....."kept the Canada going at full speed as he always had done for twenty years."

Boston, was a hub for immigration, but initially for the Irish. From 1845, following the corrupt land use policies of the British that precipitated mass starvation during the Irish Potato Famine, Boston became a magnet for Irish immigrants. In the late 19th and early 20th centuries they were joined by immigrants from Italy, Russia and other Europeans countries. While Isaac arrived in Boston in 1898, we do not know how long he stayed there.

Ellis Island (where Tillie and her siblings disembarked) has become synonymous with immigration and the Statue of Liberty, which so many gazed at hopefully and no doubt, tearfully, the enduring symbol of "Der Goldene Medina" ("The Golden Land"). Since Tillie had family already here (the Formanns), she probably did not have to linger on the island, but for many others a stay could last days, weeks or months.

Ellis Island, 1905

The Appelbaums

On Isaac Kaplan's 1908 marriage certificate, his father is listed as "Himan Kaplan" and his mother as "Eavie Appelbaum" (apple tree). The latter surname is never mentioned again, until...I found that in the 1930 US Census, a Joseph Appelbaum was living as a boarder with Isaac's daughter Fannie (Eavie Appelbaum Kaplan's granddaughter) and her husband Carl Bromberg. It's the same apartment I grew up in twenty-five years later at 4303 10th Avenue in Brooklyn, above Fannie and Carl's grocery store.

Joseph Appelbaum was a 24-year-old pharmacist working in a drug store (probably Trachtman's next door to the grocery). Additional research shows that Joseph's parents were David Appelbaum, age 62 and wife Eda, age 58. David was born in "Russia/Poland" and Eda, in NY. Joseph was the youngest sibling (brother Isidore, 29, sister Stella, 32). Joseph's paternal grandparents back in "Russia/Poland" had been Wolf Appelbaum and Fayge Rivkah Cohen, both born in ca.1840s.

Was it a coincidence that Fannie (who had paternal Appelbaum ancestors) had a boarder, also named Appelbaum? I thought that perhaps Joseph might be the "missing link" to how Appelbaums are related to Kaplans.

Months later, when I had gotten my Ancestry DNA test results, one of the DNA matches I contacted was a man named Richard Feifer. A Connecticut physician, Rich had answered my query and informed me that he was descended from a couple named Hersh Wolf and Eva Apfelbaum, Hersh's first wife. Aha!

DNA said we were third cousins, but now it seemed, we had some potential relatives in common. Rich has an extensive family tree posted on Ancestry, although the Apfelbaum branch is relatively small (Apfelbaum is the German spelling). Comparing my information about Joseph Appelbaum's ancestors and Rich's about his, I was able to draw a hypothesis that while not entirely confirmable, is I think, reasonably credible.

Rich's family was able to trace his Apfelbaum branch back to Avraham Yishrai Apfelbaum, born ca. 1820 in Bobruisk, Mogilev, Belarus (date of death is unknown), the area of Russia where the Kaplans were from. His two sons were Morris Apfelbaum and Hersh Wolf Apfelbaum (1846-1930). Not much information about Morris is available, but he was a "shammos" (caretaker) of a synagogue and is buried in Husi, Rumania. Hersh Wolf was born in Bobruisk and also died in Husi, Rumania, where he had emigrated. According to another Apfelbaum cousin, Norman Brownstein, he worked in the wholesale leather goods field and as a shoemaker. He was, "relatively well-to-do by the standard at the time."

Hersh Wolf Apfelbaum
Photo courtesy Sachs/Feifer
Family Tree

Hersh Wolf's first wife was Eva Apfelbaum, born in Sculeni, Rumania in 1849 and who died in 1875 in the childbirth of their fourth child, Rose, who was Norman and Rich's great-grandmother. She is buried in Husi. After she died, he married Fagle Apfelbaum (?-1893) and after she died, a third wife (no details). Hersh Wolf and Eva's daughter Rosie Apfelbaum (1872-1953), was Rich's great-grandmother. Rosie married Samuel Wenof and they had a daughter, Rae Ruth, who was Rich's grandmother.

The genealogy of the Apfelbaums was initially done by an Apfelbaum distant relative named Norman Sachs in 1953!

My hypothesis is that Hersh Wolf had a son, David, born 1868 (Joseph the boarder's father) with Faygle, but had somehow not found his way onto the Apfelbaum family tree. I also think that Hersh Wolf had a sister Eavie (my great-grandmother), also unlisted, who married my great-grandfather Himan Kaplan. Matching possible dates of birth backward from Joseph Appelbaum to his father David Appelbaum to his father Wolf Appelbaum on my side to Rae Ruth Apfelbaum Wenof to Rosie Apfelbaum to Hersh Wolf Apfelbaum to Avraham Yishai Apfelbaum on Rich's side, the dates align very well, generationally.

If my hypothesis is true, then Hersh Wolf Apfelbaum was my grandfather Isaac Kaplan's uncle and Joseph Appelbaum the boarder, his second cousin. Not only did Isaac's daughter Fanny take Joseph into her home (which had an extra bedroom) next to the pharmacy, but Isaac and Tillie also lived on the same block, a pretty likely example of family looking after family.

While this hypothesis seems plausible, there is no evidence to support it, although our DNA results confirm that Rich and I are related.

Tillie & Isaac Kaplan, Together

Photo of Isaac Kaplan in original frame, ca. 1930

By the time Tillie and Isaac married in 1908, all of their children, born in Russia (now Ukraine and Belarus) had been brought to America. Tillie's first husband, Yehudah Lib HaKohane had died in Russia, but Isaac's first wife Dora died in the United States. Anna knew only that she had died at a relatively early age and that she died of complications from diabetes.

At the time of their marriage on July 11, 1908, Isaac was said to be 47 and Tillie was 30 according to their marriage certificate, although those numbers vary with census forms that also vary. Their blended family consisted of Tillie's son Moses, now Morris (b. ca. 1895 and later adopted by Isaac) and Isaac's children Fannie (b. ca. 1881), Joseph (b. ca. 1893), Julius (b. ca. 1885), Yisroel (Israel, b. ca. 1878), Shmuel (Samuel, b. ca. 1895) and Benjamin (b. ca. 1891, known as Morris).

Although Tillie and Isaac got married in the Bronx, they spent the rest of their lives in Brooklyn. By the 1910 Census, they were living at 388 South 3rd St., by Isaac's 1915 naturalization paper at 494 Livonia Ave., by the 1920 Census within Assembly District 2, and by the 1930 census at 4309 10th Avenue in the neighborhood of Boro Park.

Isaac, who had been a bookbinder in Russia, was listed in the 1910 Census as working in a candy store (our mutual interest in candy confirms that we are related). In 1915, though, he is listed in his naturalization paper as a tailor and in the 1920 Census his occupation is listed as, "Fish Clergy" (I guess he sold, "Holy Mackerels"); a humorous misspelling of "clerk."

Anna recalled that after, "Isaac and Tillie married, they had a stand outside of a store on Blake Ave. in Brownsville (then an immigrant Jewish neighborhood) in Brooklyn. They sold pickles, herrings, etc. Later, they had a store on Livonia Ave. in East New York (Brooklyn). In half of the store

Anna Kaplan, left and Helen Karp, right, ca. 1920

they sold fresh fish. The other half was rented by a Mrs. Karp, who sold fresh fruits and vegetables." Anna Karp was a young widow with several children; the youngest named Helen (b. 1916). Tillie, Isaac and Anna (b. 1913) lived on the third floor (of the building) and Mrs. Karp and her family on the second floor. The business occupied the first floor."

"After that," Anna recalled, "they heard about a new development in Boro Park. It must have been new, because the streets were not paved yet. My parents took the last empty store on the block, 4309 10th Avenue. They took an apartment around the corner at 1010 43rd St., a four-family house."

Anna, Tillie and Isaac Kaplan, ca. 1920

In about 1923, the new block on which they occupied the last store contained Trachtman's Drug Store on the corner at 4301 10th Ave., step-sister and brother-in-law Fannie and Carl Bromberg's grocery at no. 4303, a tailor shop at no. 4305 (operated, Anna said by "a tall woman and a short man"), a candy store run by husband and wife Harry and Gertie at no. 4307 and at no. 4309, Tillie and Isaac's store; Tillie sold fish in one half and Isaac was in charge of fruits and vegetables in the other half (they owned the store, but not the building). Around the corner was Schertz's Bakery, still in the business of enveloping the neighborhood in the enticing aroma of fresh rye and pumpernickel when I was growing up on 10th Ave. in the 1950s (as were the drug store, grocery, candy store and tailor shop).

Left: Isaac Kaplan in front of Trachtman's Drug Store, 10th Ave., Boro Park (the dentist office was above), the block where Tillie and he had opened a store. Photo ca. 1930. Note Ex-Lax sign at right. Ex-Lax, a popular chocolate flavor laxative, was manufactured in a factory on Atlantic Avenue in downtown Brooklyn. The building was converted into co-op loft apartments in 1979. Right: Tillie Kaplan in front of drug store. Note: NYC Parks Dept. building and concrete playground in background. Behind park building is an elevated subway line (the El).

Trachtman's Drug Store (pictured above), next to the grocery/apartment where I grew up had a fascinating Communist connection that I only recently discovered. The drug store existed from at least the late 1920s to the late 1950s, when we moved from the neighborhood. My older brother Ira said that Mr. Trachtman gave him his first job as a young boy, delivering prescriptions to elderly shut-ins within a couple of blocks of the pharmacy. For that, he would get a tip of a nickel or a dime. We both remember Mr. Trachtman as a nice man; middle-aged with wire-frame eye glasses, dark gray hair and a matching thin moustache. He apparently was also involved with or sympathetic to the International Workers Order, a left-wing social services organization that had split off from the Jewish Workmen's Circle in 1930. The IWO provided low-cost health insurance, medical treatment and even cemetery privileges to its members and because the government was suspicious of its Socialist/Communist politics, members felt more comfortable dealing with businesses like Trachtman's that were connected to its causes. It dissolved in 1954 (during the "Red Scare") under pressure from New York State, which considered it too close to the Communist Party.

Isaac, who had bravely brought his entire family to America, died on Oct. 5, 1931 and is buried in Montefiore Cemetery in Springfield Gardens in Queens, NY. After his death, Tillie and Anna moved out of their four-room apartment into a three-room place at 1008 44th St. Tillie went to work in a fish store on 13thAve. nearby, (her boss Anna said, "was a real crook"). She soon met Rose Becker, who sold fish a few blocks away and the Becker family, including son Izzy and daughter Ida became lifelong friends. Tillie worked in that store until she had a heart attack and had to retire, around 1941.

Cooking Memories

When Anna was a young child, her mother Tillie made all of the family's meals from scratch, even as she worked in the store. Friday afternoons Isaac and Tillie closed the store early to prepare for Shabbat. Tillie made big dinners to welcome the Sabbath: gefilte fish (no doubt made with fish from the store), chicken soup with carrots and thin noodles made by hand, roast chicken, always a favorite and tzimmes, a stew of carrots and prunes. For dessert there was homemade apple cake or apple sauce.

On Rosh Hashonah and Yom Kippur, the store was closed and Isaac spent the whole day in shul (synagogue). Tillie also spent time at services, but not all day. On Erev Yom Kippur, just before the Kol Nidre service and the fast began for the holiday, Tillie, with Anna's help typically served an early dinner of gefilte fish (the fish were sometimes kept alive in their bathtub), soup and boiled chicken (as a kid, I remember the tasteless boiled chicken as almost adding insult to injury as we were about to begin the 24-hour Yom Kippur fast). To break the fast the next evening, they had a light meal; often pot cheese, bananas and sour cream and a piece of cake. Tillie baked her own challahs.

Tillie's English/Yiddish Pillsbury Cookbook, ca. 1940

Anna's Rosh Hashanah Teiglach Treats (for a sweet New Year)

2 cups flour
½ tsp. baking powder
2 eggs
2 tbs. oil
2 tbs. sugar, plus 1 cup sugar
1/2 lb. honey
1 lb. chopped walnuts

Mix flour with baking powder, sugar, eggs and oil. Knead a smooth dough and roll out on a floured board to ¼ inch thickness. Cut into 1-inch squares and bake on a greased cookie sheet in a moderate oven at 350, until light brown. Bring to a boil honey with 1 cup sugar and 1 lb. chopped walnuts. Add the baked cakes and stir with wooden spoon until the cakes are brown. Remove from stove top and sprinkle with 2 tbs. water. Separate teiglach and place them in a greased pie plate to cool.

Anna's mother she described as, "a remarkable woman." Anna's father, a very serious man, "was prim and proper and not the type of man to go, 'Ha, ha, ha'." He served as the shammos (caretaker) of the synagogue and taught bar mitzvah students. When he died, the synagogue paid tribute to him by redirecting the hearse to pass in front of their apartment on its way to the cemetery where he, and eventually Tillie were buried.

They celebrated the holiday of Sukkot, but did not have a sukkah in which to eat (a temporary hut with semi-open thatched roof, to see the stars), as they lived in an apartment. To celebrate Simchat Torah, Tillie and Anna climbed the long flights of stairs to the women's balcony in their shul. "The men went around with beautiful Torahs," she said, "but of course the ladies sat upstairs and never got to them." She thinks her father got to carry a Torah, because, "he was very well liked."

The celebration continued into the streets as, "men danced with Torahs...even though the streets hadn't been

paved yet. Children had flags with apples stuck in the point."
I remember similar scenes, when I was a child, forty years
later at that very same synagogue in Boro Park (although we
had paved streets by then).

Joel's Chock-Full-O-Flavor Brisket

3+ lb. brisket (second cut preferable)
1 cup regular or decaf coffee, as prepared for drinking
1 pkg. onion soup mix, regular or reduced sodium
1 cup tomato sauce, regular or reduced sodium
1 cup beef broth
½ cup ginger ale
½ cup Kosher Concord wine
1 tsp. dried oregano

Preheat oven to 325. In large roasting pan, combine coffee, tomato sauce, onion soup mix, beef broth, ginger ale, wine and oregano. Place meat in pan (do not trim fat!) and cover with gravy mixture (there is absolutely no need to sear meat first—it will have so much flavor, you'll "plotz"). Cover and cook in oven for up to 4 hours, turning brisket over after 2½ hours. Remove from oven, let cool and slice excess fat off meat. Slice against the grain and return sliced meat to the gravy in the pot. The gravy will be a deep brown color. Refrigerate overnight (always tastes better the next day). The flavor intensifies and the brisket is even softer. I've been a vegetarian for 25 years and so never eat this, but folks who do, rave about it.

At Purim, when Jewish children and adults often dress in costume today, Anna doesn't recall that as a tradition of her childhood. Hamantaschen (triangular pastries) were, though, and her mother made them with prune lekvar (fruit butter) or "mun" (poppy seed filling), which she didn't care for, but her parents liked.

Passover was a major holiday in the Kaplan household. Before the holiday, it was traditional to rid their home of even the tiniest specks of chometz (anything that contained grain). Isaac took Anna throughout the apartment utilizing a white chicken feather to brush the crumbs found in nooks and crannies into a bag. Her father then took the bag of crumbs to the shul, where they were burned. "He was extremely religious," Anna reminded me. "I told you he put on tefillin (phylacteries) every morning."

For Passover, all eight days require separate pots and pans, utensils and dishes, different from the daily separate items used for dairy or meat meals. In those days, as in our kosher home now, they would have four sets of virtually everything: meat and dairy for daily use and meat and dairy for Passover. Is it a lot of work? "Oy vey," and you can quote me on that.

Here's how Anna described how they prepared for Passover in the 1920s:

"My mother got busy with the pots and pans. We used to have a coal stove. A wonderful coal stove. It had four burners and my mother used to buff the top so that it would shine beautifully. It gave a wonderful heat. For Passover, you had to burn out the inside of the stove. My mother did the work. My father wasn't so handy around the house. My mother also did the shopping. I don't remember my father doing the shopping with her."

"She made gefilte fish—Oh, there was nothing like it. She used pike and whitefish and a piece of carp. She chopped the fish by hand. She had a bluish gray cast iron pot, with a white inside. It weighed a ton and two people had to lift it. It cooked so well because it retained the heat, so you didn't have to use a big fire. Pike and whitefish are soft, but carp is hard to chop. When you open a carp, the top is soft, but the bottom has the bones. She took the head, skin, bones and some onions and lined the bottom of the pot. Then she put sliced carrots over the onions and the fish parts. Then she mixed eggs, matzoh meal, chopped fish, onions, salt and pepper and combined it to form ovals. Then she put the ovals into the simmering stock"

Anna's Variation: Easy Baked Gefilte Fish

3 lbs. filleted white fish
1 tbs. salt
pepper to taste
1 large onion, grated
1 large carrot, grated
2 stalks celery, chopped
2 slices stale white bread,
    soaked in cold water and squeezed dry
3 eggs

Chop fish and add other ingredients in order listed and mix. Line loaf pan with foil and fill half full with fish pulp and smooth it down. Preheat oven to 350. Bake 40 minutes until brown on top. Cool, then invert pan and peel off foil. Slice and serve.

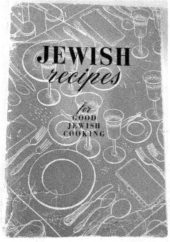

Tillie's English/Yiddish Cookbook, publ. 1940

At a typical seder, Anna's relatives came up from Philadelphia (brothers Philip & Morris Morrison and their families).

"My father," she added, "used to get the wine. We didn't make any, but there were people who made their own. Concord wine only. We used 'Rogers 1847' silverware, a white linen table cloth with a design, brass candlesticks, white oval china platters with scalloped edges and plain white dishes. The matzoh cover was old and beige. It must have been my father's from his first marriage."

Anna helped Tillie make potato kugel (baked pudding), tzimmes, chicken soup with matzoh balls, pot roast, roast chicken and Passover rolls.

Anna's Tasty Passover Rolls

2 cups matzoh meal
1 tsp. salt
1 tbs. sugar
1 cup water
½ cup oil (peanut preferred, but not necessary)
4 eggs

Combine matzoh meal, sugar and salt. Bring oil and water to boil. Add matzoh meal mixture and mix well. Beat in eggs, one at a time. Let stand 15 minutes. With oiled hands, shape into rolls and place on well-greased cookie sheet. Bake at 375 degrees for 50 minutes. Makes 12. Delicious, but a dozen is never enough!

Tillie and later Anna, purchased chickens at a live chicken market on 13th Ave. and 39th St. "You used to go in and pick out a chicken that you thought you'd like. They were all in cages," she explained. "The mashgiach (kosher supervisor) was there and he'd slaughter them (behind a wall). They'd pluck the chicken by hand. They would cut it into the parts you wanted and then give you the insides. You'd bring it home and then kasher it (soak and salt it and then put it on a tilted board so that the blood would drain into the sink)."

I remember going with Anna to the live chicken market in the mid '50s. It was still in business and a trolley line ran down 39th St. Who can forget the occasional headless chicken who escaped from the back after the mashgiach did his deed. Maybe that's why I'm a vegetarian.

During Passover Anna recalled, "My father was very religious, so we couldn't use green peas or string beans (an Ashkenazic/Eastern European Jewish custom)," she added. Seltzer was the beverage and for dessert, "we used to have fresh fruit and compote (cooked fruit)."

At the Passover seder, Anna's father sat at the head of the table, in a chair with two arms. In back of him was a big white pillow (it is a custom to lean back on a pillow during the seder to emphasize that Jews are no longer slaves now, so can rest comfortably). He conducted the seder in Hebrew, without any English, as he didn't speak English, but her mother did.

"My father hid the afikomen (matzoh that children are supposed to find for a prize), but I could never find it. You had to say the whole thing (Haggadah narrative) from beginning to end. No skipping! In between, when eating, the family discussed what was doing in Europe or in America. To tell you the truth, it was not very exciting; not like you do with different things (our family tradition is to sing Hebrew songs, song parodies, tell stories and act out little plays, among other "shtick")."

"After the seder, my two aunts (from Philadelphia, both named Fannie) helped clear the table. My mother had baked sponge cake and honey cake. We had that with tea. No coffee, because you can't drink coffee with milk (at a meat meal), God forbid!"

"When the door was opened for Elijah (the custom of welcoming the prophet), I was so scared. I opened the door and went on the other side, away from the door. I used to look at the wine cup for Elijah, to see if he drank any."

63

Anna's Angelic Passover Sponge Cake

9 eggs
1 cup sugar
¾ cup potato flour
½ cup matzoh meal
1 lemon rind and juice

Put egg whites in bowl and beat with sugar a little at a time until stiff. Add whole egg yolks all at once and beat until you can't see any yellow. Add lemon rind and juice. Beat and add potato flour and last, add matzoh meal. Put into ungreased 10-inch tube pan and cut through with knife several times to release air bubbles. Bake slowly at 325 for 1 hour. Take from oven and let cool and then turn upside down.

The Kaplan Siblings

Carl and Fannie Bromberg, ca. 1910 above, ca. late 1940s below

At their 1908 marriage, Tillie and Isaac's new family consisted of Tillie's son Morris and Isaac's children Fannie, Joseph, Julius, Yisroel (Israel), Shmuel (Samuel) and Benjamin (known as Morris). Anna felt closest to her older sister Fannie, who was in her early thirties, married and a parent when Anna was born. Fannie and her husband Carl Bromberg (affectionately known as Bunky) owned a grocery store at 4303 10th Ave. in Boro Park. She and Carl had two children; Anna's niece Ethel, with whom she remained close and nephew Oscar. Both were older than she and when she was born in 1913, Anna became an instant aunt.

In the 1915 NYS Census, both Fannie and Carl are listed as "aliens." He is age 37 and she, 33. Their children are Etta (Ethel), six and Oscar, three. Carl is a grocer, while Fannie does "housework." At the 1920 US Census they are living on Hinsdale St. in Brooklyn and still grocers. Carl's date of immigration is listed as 1900 and Fannie's as 1902. Both do not speak English. In the 1925 NYS Census, they are listed as having lived in the US 25 years and they now reside at 4303 10th Ave. in the apartment above their grocery store (later occupied by my family). The 1930 US Census informs us that Fannie's age at marriage was 27 and her immigration year, 1904. Carl is 52; Fannie, 49; Ethel, 21 and Oscar, 18. Ethel is listed as a bookkeeper in a "dress house" (probably Lerner's) and Oscar as helping out in the grocery.

Photo left: Ethel and Fannie Bromberg. Photo right: Anna Kaplan and Oscar Bromberg, both photos in front of 4303 10th Ave., Fannie and Carl's grocery store, ca. 1930

After Carl died Fannie moved in with Ethel and her husband Lou Golden to a three-bedroom apartment in a more middle-class area of Boro Park. My family then moved into their apartment above the grocery. Fannie was close to her stepmother Tillie, as well as to Anna and after Tillie's death I think took on more of a maternal role and became substitute grandmother to us. She was well into her seventies when I was a little boy and lived to about 94. Although by then, she spoke English well, she always endearingly called me the diminutive of either my English name (Joeleh) or my Yiddish name (Yosseleh). Few people of that generation spoke Hebrew, but many men learned to read it in preparation for their Bar Mitzvahs (there were no Bat Mitvahs for girls, then) and it was used exclusively in synagogue services (most Ashkenazic Jews were Orthodox and services in those days contained virtually no English).

When Anna had one of several surgeries when we were children, I stayed with Ethel, Lou and Fannie, while Ira stayed in Queens with Louis's older brother Alex and his wife Lillian. Fannie and Ethel were gracious hosts. Of all of her nieces, Anna was closest to Ethel. They were more like sisters and Ethel was special to us all.

Anna Kaplan and her niece, Ethel Bromberg, ca. 1935

Ethel and Lou were always wonderful to us. Ethel was lively and Lou was quiet. He managed a large shoe store and whenever we would visit with our parents, he'd greet us with, "What size shoe do you wear?" For Ira and me the answer varied as we grew into young men, but Lou's response was always the same. He'd disappear into his magic shoe closet and pull out a pair of brand new dress shoes for each of us (somehow, he always had our sizes). Shoes were expensive then, and his generosity was appreciated.

Photo left: Ethel and Lou Golden wedding picture.
Photo right: Ethel and Lou 50th wedding anniversary

Fannie and Carl Bromberg, Ethel and Lou Golden, Eileen and Samuel Golden, ca. 1940s

Fannie and Carl's son Oscar became a math teacher. When he was drafted into the Army during World War ll he was stationed in Hawaii, where he taught on base during the war. Anna frequently corresponded with him. When he returned to the States, he gave her his military issue Hebrew Bible which had been distributed to all Jewish soldiers. After Anna died and I was going through her things, I found it. She had saved it all those years. Recently, as a result of this family history, I began a correspondence with Oscar's daughter Debbi (who I have not seen in over fifty years), a former nurse now living in North Carolina and raising goats on their farm with her husband. I mailed Debbi her father's bible, which she was so happy to receive.

Besides Fannie, the other Kaplan sibling we saw on a regular basis was Anna's older brother Julius and his wife Rae. They also owned a grocery store, on Ave. M in a Brooklyn neighborhood called Midwood. By the time I knew him, Julius was elderly and had emphysema, rarely acknowledged us kids and never left their apartment above the store. According to the 1930 US Census, Julius's occupation was house painter and he was born ca. 1885. He was 14 years older than Rae, who was American-born. Their children were Jack (Jerry) age 10 and Edward, age five. The family lived at 2351 81 St. in Brooklyn. In his naturalization papers Julius was born on June 29, 1886 and arrived in the US on March 19, 1902 on the ship Graf Waldersee, which sailed from Hamburg, Germany. His occupation was listed as (wall)paper hanger and 304 E. 2nd St (the grocery fronted Ave. M) was the family's home.

Rae and Julius had two sons: Jerry, who managed the grocery and Eddie, who went to medical school in Switzerland and became a doctor in Winsted, CT. Eddie had served in the army during WW ll, and his unit was one of the forces that entered Berlin at the end of the war. He had told my brother Ira that his platoon had entered Hitler's Berlin

Julius Kaplan, ca. 1915

headquarters, where they found his office walls covered in fine leather. The American GIs stripped the walls of the leather, cut it into small pieces and took it with them as souvenirs. Eddie said he had a pair of boots made from Hitler's leather wall coverings. I can't corroborate the story, but it is an amazing one.

Rae spent long hours on her feet in the grocery downstairs, managing it with their son, Jerry. She had a hard life and one way she dealt with it was by constantly cursing and making sarcastic comments. She truly had a heart of gold, though, and loved our visits. We would often have Sunday dinner there and because she did not keep kosher and my father did, she would only serve cold dairy meals. I once asked my father why he ate there on dishes that had been used to serve non-kosher meats previously (nobody used paper plates then) and he replied that he appreciated Rae's efforts and would never insult her by refusing to eat her food.

Photo left: Rae and Julius Kaplan, ca. 1970.

Rae gave Ira and me the treat of picking any candy or snack item in the store to take upstairs. Potato chips, she referred to as, "Potato Shits." We were often given the assignment of fishing for submerged pickles in the large wooden barrel that was kept in the store. We had to push aside the creepy pale green slime called "schimmel" in Yiddish that was so thick that even sonar wouldn't have been able to pierce it. Rae worked in that store until nearly the day she died.

Morris, born Benjamin, was the financial success of the Kaplan siblings and was also a very fine person. According to the CT Death Index, Morris was born on January 29, 1889 and died on July 9, 1969 in Bloomfield, CT. His naturalization papers stated that his birth name was Mottale and that he arrived in America on April 5, 1902, sailing from Rotterdam, the Netherlands under the name Maitch (which Anna always called him) Kaplan on the ship, Graf Waldersee. His wife Rebecca (Becky) Kamins was born in 1890 and they married on July 4, 1914. At the time, they lived at 402 Hillside Ave. in Hartford and his naturalization papers were dated June 27, 1933.

In Morris's draft registration form of 1917, he is listed as a "merchant baker" and lived at 16 Bedford Ave. in Hartford as a registered alien. In the 1920 US census, Morris is described as a driver for a bakery. His age is 28 and Becky's as 32, although previously she had been reported as a year younger than he (family lore had always considered Becky a few years older than her husband). By the 1940 US census, Morris had achieved the status of drug store owner, the occupation I had always associated with him, although he was retired by the time I was a child.

Morris's drug store was in a Jewish neighborhood of Hartford. Among his customers was the young Abe Ribicoff, who went on to a distinguished career as Pres. Kennedy's Sec. of

Morris Kaplan and sons Henry and Alex in his Hartford, CT drug store, ca. 1940

Health, Education and Welfare, as well as service as a US Senator from Connecticut. Morris was a gregarious man, always with a cigar in his mouth. He ran the soda fountain and commercial goods of the drug store, which brought him in daily contact with his customers.

We visited Becky and Morris over the years at their home in West Hartford and then Bloomfield; a trip that took over three hours from Brooklyn and brought us past fields of tobacco, an important Connecticut crop at that time. Morris was always happy to see all of us, and like Fannie, was very fond of Anna, whom he referred to as his "kid" sister.

Morris's grandson Robert Kaplan remembers him fondly: "He spoiled us boys (his three brothers, as well) with constant licorice, ice cream and gifts....He was incredibly kind and loving to us."

Becky and Morris had two sons; Alex, born in 1916 and Henry in 1919. Alex had graduated from Columbia University and was a pharmacist and later, pharmaceutical sales rep. Alex's daughter Deb Brindis said of her father, "He was such a fun person. Absolutely hilarious."

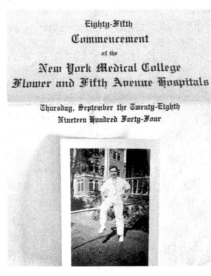

Eighty-Fifth
Commencement
of the
New York Medical College
Flower and Fifth Avenue Hospitals

Thursday, September the Twenty-Eighth
Nineteen Hundred Forty-Four

Henry Kaplan medical school graduation program and photo addition, 1944.

Henry became a leading ob/gyn in Connecticut, living and practicing in New Britain. He and his wife Rhoda also had a house on the shore in Clinton, CT.

There was a large Roman Catholic church across the street from Morris Kaplan's drugstore and he had become close friends with the priest, Father John Dooley. According to Morris's grandson Robert, Father Dooley came into the drugstore each day for coffee and to smoke cigars with Morris. He was a respected and influential figure in the Kaplan family, encouraging Henry to attend local Catholic school Trinity College, which he did. Anna had told me that Henry served as a pall bearer at Father Dooley's funeral mass.

Henry Kaplan couldn't make Anna and Louis's wedding. He was serving in the Army, stationed in the Philippines. He sent a radiogram.

RADIOGRAM
GLOBE WIRELESS

SFB 632 CC INTL MANILA 116 56 122 JAN 11 1947 NFT

1947 JAN 11 AM 5 40

EFM MISS A KAPLAN
4611 10THAVE
BROOKLYN
NEWYORK

CONGRATULATIONS. LASTING HAPPINESS TO YOU BOTH.
MY THOUGHTS ARE WITH YOU. BEST WISHES TO ALL AT HOME

Barbara and I had visited Henry and Rhoda once, several years before we moved to Connecticut. Around dinner time, Henry said enthusiastically, "Do you guys like grinders?" We looked at him with dumb expressions on our faces. He patiently described a grinder and we blurted out, "Ya mean a hero? Of course, we like heroes."

It took a while to understand "Connecticutese." A year or two later, when we moved to New London in southeastern Connecticut, our landlord told us that his family owned several "package stores." We thought he meant UPS stores, unbeknownst to us that package stores were liquor stores. And old-time New Londoners referred to soda as "pop." Plus, New London was Red Sox territory.

Morris Kaplan was also the name of Tillie's son, adopted by Isaac. In our family, we differentiated the two with the titles, "Morris from Brownsville" and "Morris from Hartford." The former was born in Tarashcha about 1895 and on the manifest of the ship he arrived on in 1906, he is listed as a nine-year old

Morris and Gertie Kaplan, ca. 1940

named Moses. He married Gertrude (Gertie) Rosenthal and they settled in Brownsville, Brooklyn. They had two children, Lillian and Joseph. I knew Morris only as an older man who wore a derby, smoked a cigar and worked in a candy store.

Lillie and Anna were very close and she visited us often. She married Samuel Goodman (Guttman) and they in turn, had two children; Paulette and Michael. Lillie was a very thoughtful person and when she told a story, it always seemed to end with a surprise; to her, as well. Sam was a quiet, pipe-smoking intellectual and worked in the Post Office. He had a brother who was a diplomat in Germany.

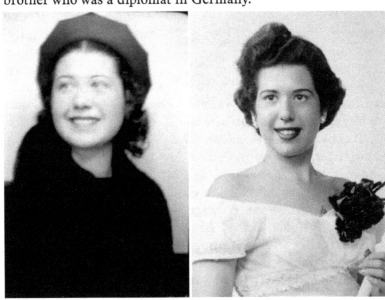

Lillian Goodman, left ca. 1945 and daughter Paulette Goodman, ca. 1958

Anna's brother Joseph Kaplan was the sibling I was named after and therefore as per Jewish custom, had died before I was born. Because he died relatively young and due to the superstitions of the time, my middle name of Stanley is based on an obscure cousin in the Old Country who was reputed to have lived to a very old age.

I knew little about Joseph, except what I had gleaned from census reports. In the NYS census of 1915, he is listed as age 32, his wife Celia is 31 and they have two children: Nathan (Nat), four and Arthur (Archie), six months old (a third son Philip was born ca. 1925). He's a house painter and the family lives on Hinsdale St. in Brownsville, Brooklyn, a street we see often in family addresses. His year of immigration is listed as 1900. By the 1940 US census, Joseph and Celia are living in Amityville, NY (Joseph died in 1942; Celia in 1970).

That lack of knowledge changed dramatically, when as this book was at the printer, I received an Ancestry message from Joanne Kaplan Handloser, who had just gotten her DNA results and found that we are second cousins. Not only that, but we are both named after Joseph, who was her grandfather. Joanne sent photos and filled me in on a bit of her family history.

Left photo: Celia and Joseph Kaplan, ca. 1910s.
Right photo: Nat, Archie and Celia Kaplan, ca. 1920s

Her father Arthur (Archie) was Joseph and Celia's son and her uncles were Nat and Philip. Archie was a store manager, Nat worked as a civilian for the Navy and Philip was a salesman. Joanne and her husband retired as NYC ad agency executives.

I remembered that Aunt Celia had attended my Bar Mitzvah, but did not know her well. Joanne remembers her grandmother fondly: "Her English was limited and she spoke with her sons in Yiddish. We played cards (she won) and we watched the Lawrence Welk Show and Perry Como (who she called Perela)."

Anna's older brother Yisroel (Israel) Kaplan, according to the 1930 US Census, was born ca. 1878 in Russia and immigrated in 1903. He was a custom tailor who had his own shop and married to a woman named Myra (Mollie). They had two children; Louis, who was married to Maddie and Sarah, who was married to a man named Charles Levy. Yisroel and his family lived in Ellenville in the Catskills. I don't remember him, at all, but I have a faint recollection of his children, as adults.

Left: Yisroel (Israel) Kaplan, ca. 1920. Right: Lou Kaplan
with wife Maddie on left and Ethel Bromberg on right, ca. 1920s

Another sibling, Shmulka (Samuel) was born ca. 1895. Anna said he lived with a number of women and his first wife was possibly, Dora. She remembered his second wife as Ida. He was a house painter and we did not see him very often. He was known for having a taste for liquor and not holding it very well. That reputation led Anna to ask her sister-in-law Rae Kaplan to forewarn him (Rae was pretty tough and plain spoken) that he was to watch his intake and behavior at my Bar Mitzvah, where there was an open bar (presumably, he hadn't at Ira's a year earlier). Apparently, he got the message.

The Cousins

One of Tillie's relatives who used to visit our family when we were kids was an older widow, whom we knew as, "Cousin Lakeh." Her real name was Lena Sklar. She was very nice, but spoke little English. She had been born in Russia ca. 1884 and in 1940 lived at 463 Hinsdale St. in Brooklyn with her 56-year-old husband Sam, a laborer, and a boarder.

Anna used to tell us that she and her late husband had been so in love, that they always ate their meals from the same plate! Sometimes she varied the story so that they had been so poor that they only owned one plate. Either way it mystified me that Cousin Lakeh was so poor and in love that all they had in their home was a single plate. Even Romeo and Juliet probably had service for six.

Another distant relative was an elderly woman called, "Faigel der Grinner (Fannie the Greenhorn)". She was always referred to by that Yiddish nickname. Apparently, of her generation, she was the last to immigrate to America (decades earlier) and so no matter how old she was or how long she lived here (and she spoke English reasonably well), she was still the family's greenhorn (new arrival).

One cousin who figured prominently in Anna and Louis's wedding was Abe Constantine (Abraham Costantin). Like many of her mother Tillie's relatives, Abe was a musician who led the band at their wedding. In the 1940 US Census, it was stated that he was born in Russia, ca. 1892 and lived with his wife Rose and daughters Yetta and Gertrude in a house they owned at 1910 85th St. (valued at $7,000) in Brooklyn.

Anna remembered them fondly:

"They were a very friendly, very nice family. They lived on 85th St. in Bensonhurst and each family visited the other. Anna Constantine married a man from Brooklyn and then moved to Trenton (New Jersey). We visited them when you were a child."

Apparently Yetta had changed her name to Anna by that time. Who can blame her.

Anna remembered a cousin named Rosenthal, but could not recall his first name. He was either a foreign correspondent or a local reporter, she thought, in the 1940s for the "New York Journal-American" daily newspaper. He was a bachelor, she said, who lived in Manhattan, but "had a sister who lived on 15th Ave. in Brooklyn, and picked up his laundry there."

"Rosenthal," she said, "told very interesting, just wonderful stories."

I've researched several prominent journalists named Rosenthal, but they do not match the dates, nor the newspaper as Anna had remembered.

Anna Kaplan's Story

My mother Anna was born on July 5, 1913, the only child of Tillie and Isaac Kaplan and a generation younger than her step-siblings.

Anna Kaplan birth certificate, b. 7/5/13

She was a sickly child and around the age of 12 developed tuberculosis. A traditional treatment in those days was to send the patient away to either a sanitarium or for a stay on a farm in the country. It was believed that "fresh air" and a wholesome rural environment would heal this contagious respiratory disease, so common in the cramped quarters of the cities. Anna was sent to live with a farm family in the town of South Fallsburg in the Catskills. Mr. and Mrs. Cohen were friends of Tillie and Isaac and although they were nice to Anna, the experience of separation had an indelible effect on her.

Her early years, of course, were spent in Brooklyn. Anna grew up in Boro Park and was a bright child, being in the "Rapid Advance" program at PS 131 on Ft. Hamilton Parkway (my older brother Ira and I also attended that school). After elementary school, she attended John J. Pershing Junior High School (my first art teaching position was in that school) and then New Utrecht High School, where she received a General Diploma.

After graduation, her first job was at the Venida Net Co, where she packaged the hair nets for shipping. Anna did not see a future in hair nets, so she spoke to her niece Ethel Bromberg, who in turn spoke to her boss and Anna soon joined Ethel on the clerical staff of Lerner's, a large women's fashion shop in the City. She worked with Ethel, Jessica Smith (whose father was a dress designer) and Adele Wagner (who set Anna up on a blind date with future husband Louis Levitt) and they all became close friends. Anna liked her job and colleagues and worked her way up to become a comptometer operator (a precursor of adding machines) and did that until she left to get married in 1947. That was her last paying job.

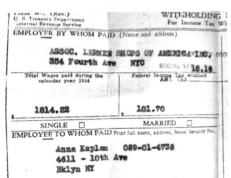

Anna's W-2 form. She earned $1,814 and 22 cents working fulltime in all of 1944

Anna Kaplan (front right in black coat) and Lerner co-workers

Lerner's was a family business founded in 1918 (in 1995 it became New York and Company) by Samuel Lerner, son of Jewish immigrants from Ukraine. The Lerner family, Anna recalled was, "not very friendly" to their employees, at least not the clerical staff.

One of the Lerner sons was Alan Jay Lerner (born the year the store was founded), who Anna emphasized was, "stuck up, stuck up." Despite that double character fault (he must have had others, as he was married eight times!), Lerner went on to become one of the great lyricists of the American theatre.

Together with composer Frederick Loewe, the team produced many of Broadway's most beloved musicals, including "Brigadoon" (1947), "Paint Your Wagon" (1951), "My Fair Lady" (1956) and "Camelot" (1961). Lerner won three Tony Awards and three Oscars. Needless to say, Anna was not impressed.

Alan Jay Lerner (left) and Frederick Loewe (right)

Louis Levitt's Story

My father Louis Levitt was the son of immigrants Sarah Czenzov (Shenzov) and Jacob Levitt, and on July 2, 1911 became the first of their children to be born in America.

Little is factually known about Sarah (b. ca. 1884, d. 4/28/58) and Jacob (b. ca. 4/10/80, d. 8/24/50) before they emigrated. They had lived in or near Vitebsk, a city in what is now Belarus. Louis had said that Sarah's family were bakers and Jacob, apparently a bricklayer. Sarah, it appears, had three sisters and her family had a farm. We do not know whether Jacob had siblings, but families were generally large in those days, so it is doubtful that he was an only child. Neither my father Louis, nor his younger brother Hy, though, ever referred to having aunts and uncles either in the US or Russia.

Envelopes addressed to "Yacob Levitt" in 1933 and "Levitts" in 1935 have survived (in poor condition), and seemingly, without their contents. The former was mailed from Vitebsk (Sarah and Jacob's hometown) by someone named Gema Yazmir. The latter was sent from Velizh (Venizh) in the Smolensk area of western Belarus by an A. M. Chernov. The envelopes were saved by Louis's older sister Elinor (born in Vitebsk), so they must have had some kind of personal meaning. Perhaps Yazmir and Chernov were siblings of either Sarah or Jacob and wrote under their married names. That's a mystery that right now remains unsolved.

Envelopes from Gena (shortened version of Evgeniy) Yazmir (top), 1933 and A. M. Chernov (center), 1935. The former was sent from Vitebsk and the latter from Velizh (Venizh) in Belarus.

I. Сибры	Про...	...	Адносіны	Месца праца	Цэх	УВАГА
1						
2						
3						

Name and address of Gena Yazmir on back of form, photo right. It is a "trydovaya knizhka," according to one translator: a personnel form asking for First Name, Last Name, Age, etc. We don't know its significance. Perhaps Gena Yazmir was looking for assistance to emigrate, or perhaps paper was scarce in Vitebsk 1933 and he just wrote on the back of a form, because it was available. No document was found in the Chernov envelope

Above Left: Unidentified woman and baby. Right: Is it possible that this is the same woman from photo left, years later? She has a similar serious visage, broad nose and hairline and the long black shawl is tied the same way in both photos. Left (back of left photo): The translation is that the photo was taken at Rafael Artistic Photography in Velizh, Belarus.
The envelope and its missing contents sent by A.M. Chernov in 1935 to the Levitts was also mailed from Velizh. So, who are the woman and baby and what is their

connection to the Chernovs and the Levitts? I'm going to go out on a limb here and suggest that maybe the photo (saved by Elinor Levitt Axelrod for decades) is possibly of Elinor as a baby with one of her grandmothers (it would have to date from ca.1905). Perhaps it is Jacob's mother holding the baby, as he had Velizh listed as his birthplace on his 1942 US draft card. Also, the photo above right was sent in the Chernov envelope in 1935 and may be of Elinor's grandmother 30 years later. Just a theory.

Jacob Levitt 1942 Draft Registration Card. Note in center right of card that under, "Place of Birth," Veliz (Velizh) is listed, not Vitebsk or Ostrovets. Vilezh is a city in the Smolensk region of Ukraine, where a letter was sent to Jacob in 1935 by AM Chernov.

Up until the translation was recently provided of Jacob Levitt's passport, no one alive today knew the name of his father. The 1907 passport, though, provides an answer, referring to Jacob (Yankel Levit---one "t"), age 27, as the son of Leib Levit. My father Louis's Hebrew name was Leib, so he was named after his grandfather. Our oldest daughter Lia's Hebrew name is Liba and she is named after her grandfather, Louis. It is likely that Leib Levitt died (see Paul Levitt's note later in the narrative for the tragic circumstances) between when Sarah and Jacob's oldest son (Alex) was born, ca. 1907 and Louis's birth in 1911, as it would have been customary to name the former after a recently deceased grandfather, rather than wait until the possibility of another son.

The folks who volunteered translations of the passport also engaged in some online debate as to what else it contained. Apparently, they agreed that it lists Jacob (Yankel) as a member of the "meschanin," or petty bourgeois, a lower middle-class group. One respondent argued that that is misleading, since the group refers not to class but to one's tax status (there is agreement, though, that Jacob paid a passport tax of 15 rubles). Meschanin, it is stated, belonged to the lowest echelon of townspeople, as opposed to the lowest level of rural folk: peasants.

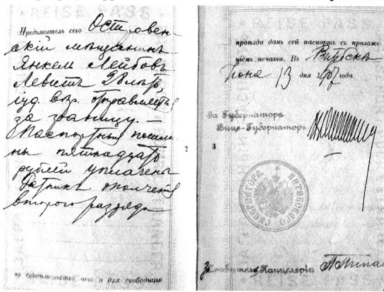

First two pages in Jacob Levitt's (Yankel Levit) passport, 1907

Last page of Jacob Levitt's 1907 passport. This is an exit visa form dated 6/18/07 from the port of Libau, now the city of Liepaja in Latvia. The ticket was stamped by the Governor of Vitebsk Province to "Ostrovets petty bourgeois Yankel, son of Leib Levit." The translator believes that Jacob (Yankel) may have originally been from the town of Ostrovets, now known as Astravyets, or his father Leib may have come from there.

Jacob's possible hometown has been translated as Ostrovets, now known as Astravyets in Belarus. Astravyets, with over 8,000 inhabitants, is today a community of controversy, through no fault of its own. It was selected by the Belorussian government to be the site of the country's first nuclear power plant. In the time of Leib Levitt, it was a village called Ostrovets. In 1872 a railroad was built linking major cities Vilna (now in Lithuania) to Minsk (now in Belarus) and Ostrovets was connected to a small station nearby by a horse-drawn railway. According to the 1887 Russian census, Ostrovets had 34 households, 248 residents, a school, a bakery (perhaps Sarah worked there), two dairy stores, a mill, a tavern, a distillery, a sawmill and a brick production company (perhaps Jacob worked there). In 1921, the Jewish population was 100.

We do not know whether Leib Levitt was definitely from Ostrovets, but settled in Vitebsk or whether Jacob Levitt was from there, as well. Sarah and Jacob were both considered "designated residents" of Ostrovets on their passports, even though they lived in Vitebsk at the time.

Recently, though, another document was found online, that points strongly to a more specific birthplace for Jacob. His 1942 US Draft Registration card lists Veliz (Velizh) under "Place of Birth." By 1942, Jacob must have understood and spoken a fair amount of English, as he had been in the US for 35 years and had his own business, so he had to have furnished the name, "Veliz" to the clerk who filled out the form.

Vilezh is one of eleven "raoins" (districts) that comprise the Vitebsk "gubernia" (region) of Belarus. It is a town of about 7,500, but in Jacob's time it was a larger community. In the 1897 Russian census (a decade before Jacob emigrated) it had a population of 12,180, of which 5,982 people were listed as Jews, comprising 49.1% of the total population. Like many communities, it has a bloody past.

It was the scene of one of the most notorious and long-lasting "blood libel" cases in modern history. Forty-three Jewish inhabitants of Velizh were arrested on ritual murder charges and kept imprisoned until the Russian Senate dropped the charges 12 years later, in 1835. Still, Czar Nicholas stated upon their release, "I do not have and indeed cannot have the inner conviction that the murder has not been committed by Jews."

View of Velizh on banks of the Dvina River. Undated, probably late 19th century. The Church of St. Elijah is in the distance.

The Jews of Vilezh no doubt, never forgot that case. Jacob, himself, it is said, had referred to pogroms later in the century, as a reason for leaving Russia.

While we don't know that Jacob and Sarah personally experienced a pogrom, they most likely had heard of the vicious Kishinev Pogrom of 1903, whose repercussions reached across the Pale of Settlement and into America. Its violence and cruelty were so great, that when the National Association for the Advancement of Colored People (NAACP) was founded in 1909, the Kishinev Pogrom was referenced in its original documents.

Whether the city of Vitebsk or the towns of Ostrovets or Velizh, Jacobs's possible birthplace (and Sarah's as well, as people in those days had neither the cultural attitude nor the means or transportation availability to travel distances to meet their potential spouses) was within that area of Belarus.

Just as Jacob's passport gave us for the first time the first name of his father, Leib, Sarah's passport also gave us the first name of her father, that had been previously unknown to my generation of Levitts. It was Yosel: the same as my Yiddish name. So now, we have two complete names of my great grandfathers: Leib Levitt and Yosel Czenzov. Unfortunately, still missing are the names of my grandmothers, as both Jewish men and women were identified in those days by their Hebrew/ Yiddish names, which are patrilineal.

The Levitt Family. Standing: Sarah, Alex, Louis, Shirley, Hyman.
Seated: Jacob, Elinor, ca. 1928

Vitebsk was also the birthplace of the beloved Russian Jewish painter Marc Chagall (1889-1985). Chagall was greatly influenced by the Hassidic tradition that flourished in the Jewish communities of Vitebsk. His paintings are full of floating lovers and fiddlers on the roof and a warm, deeply rooted love and nostalgia for his hometown.

In 1918, Chagall was appointed Commissar of Fine Arts for Vitebsk and soon founded an art academy. His stay was relatively brief, for the politics in the region were undergoing seismic changes and Chagall left for Paris, where he established his career. It is highly unlikely that within Vitebsk's large Jewish community, Sarah and Jacob had known Marc Chagall. Perhaps they knew of him in later life, as a fellow native child of Vitebsk, and its most famous and creative citizen.

Chagall, "Over Vitebsk," 1918

In terms of its Jewish history, a handful of Jews began to settle in Vitebsk in the late 16th century, several decades after it had been burned to the ground by soldiers of Ivan the Terrible. Like much of the area, the town shifted from Lithuanian to Polish to Russian control over the centuries. As Vitebsk grew into the largest city in northeast Belarus, the Jewish

Vitebsk, with main synagogue in center.

population grew, as well. By the late 19th century, 80 percent of workers in trade and industry were Jewish and Jews were involved in the areas of lumber, furniture manufacturing and brick making, among others. By 1904, 50 percent of the city's population was Jewish.

The religious, Zionist and artistic communities of Jews also flourished in the late 19th and early 20th centuries. In 1918, though, due in part to the disruption of the Russian Revolution, anti-Semitic acts increased in the area.

Before World War ll, there were 50,000 Jews living in the Vitebsk area. In 1941 the German Army completely took over the city, after the Russian Red Army retreated, the latter burning large swaths of the city as they fled. The Nazis committed atrocities beyond comprehension and description. And when the city was liberated in 1944, no Jews remained.

Between the poverty, pogroms, highwaymen, cholera epidemics (more than half a million people in Russia died of the disease between 1900-1925) and the threat of being drafted into the Czar's army, life was extremely precarious. Jacob made the courageous and difficult transatlantic journey in 1907 on the ship, SS Lituania and settled in Brooklyn.

Above: The Lituania (1889) had been named the Kina when it sailed under the East Asiatic Company, then was renamed and transferred to the Baltic America Line in 1907.

Left: Boarding pass for Jacob Levitt (Yankel Levit) on the SS Lituania, 7/1/07, sailing from Libau, now in Latvia and called Liepaja. Until 1914, Libau was a major port of the Russian Empire, since it was ice-free year-round.

Sarah, Elinor and Alex emigrated on April 27, 1910 and were listed in their passport as Sora Liba (Sarah's Yiddish name),

Elke, age five and Elie, age three (on the French pages, the language of passports at the time.)

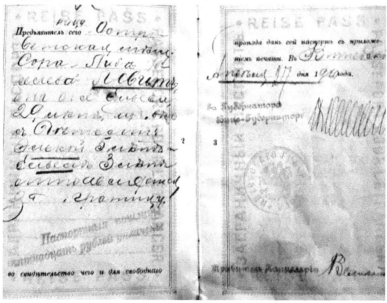

Opening pages of Sarah (Sora Liba) Levitt's passport, dated April 27, 1910.

They came on the SS George Washington out of Bremen, Germany. The ship had been launched in 1908 and was designed by the North Germany Lloyd line to carry 2679 passengers, half of them in steerage. The ship was taken over by the US in 1917 and renamed the USS George Washington and generally was in service until it was decommissioned in 1947.

S. S. George Washington

I cannot imagine what it must have been like for Sarah, with two young children, to travel alone in steerage among over 1300 other immigrants. Plus, she had to have traveled to northern Germany from Belarus to board the ship. She certainly showed courage.

Left: Inspection card listing Sora Liba Levit (Sarah Levitt). Card was stamped at the US Consulate in Bremen, Germany and by the US Public Health and Hospital Service at Ellis Island on 5/20/10. On the back of the card it warns, "Keep this Card to avoid detention at Quarantine and on Railroads in the United States." Right: Inspection card listing Yankel Levit (Jacob Levitt), a 1907 precursor of the above form for Sora Liba Levit (Sarah Levitt). The same warning is on the back of the card.

Louis Levitt, ca. 1940

My father Louis Levitt was born in Brooklyn on July 2, 1911, but in 1931 when he needed his birth certificate (no. 21580, dated 5/19/1911) for an official purpose (maybe a driver's license), he noticed that his name, as well as those of his parents had been officially misspelled and much to his surprise, he was now "Leon Leavitt." Since his parents did not speak English at the time of his birth, whoever took down the information (it looks like, "J. Black, MD") at Jewish Hospital, wrote what he heard, rather than what was said. His father's age was listed as 30 at the time and his occupation as laborer. Both parents' last names were listed as, "Leavitt" and they lived at 241 Moore St. in Brooklyn. Sarah's birth name was listed as "Ksendsoff," a phonetic interpretation of Czenzov. My father had to go to court to legally change his name back to Louis Levitt, the name he had been born with.

Louis Levitt Birth Certificate.
Note "Leon Leavitt"

The 1910 US Census has a 30-year-old married (six years) Yiddish-speaking man named Jacob Levitt living as a boarder with a Guttman family on McRebbew St. in Brooklyn. He is listed as a plasterer. Jacob's immigration year is incorrectly said to be 1908. It was common for men to emigrate first, without their spouses and children and live with other immigrant families as boarders. Anna also said that when she was a child, boarders lived with her family. Oftentimes these boarders were relatives or "landsmen," folks who were from the same town as the families they stayed with.

Landsmanshaftn, organizations of immigrants from the same town or city were a necessity for many immigrants. Many of these groups offered death and burial benefits and leased sections of cemeteries for the benefit of the poor immigrant population.

In the 1920 US census, Sarah and Jacob lived at 83 Siegel St. in Brooklyn with their children, Annie (Elinor) age 14, Alec (Alex) age 13, Louis age 8, Sadie (Shirley) age 7 and Hyman age 6. Jacob and Sarah were listed as ages 38 and 36, respectively. Jacob was described as a plasterer by occupation.

The NYS Census of 1925 finds them the owners of 837 Park Ave. in Brooklyn. They are listed as Jake, 42; Sarah, 42; Elenor (sic), 19; Alex, 18; Louie, 13; Sadie (Shirley), 12 and Hyman, 11.

Jake is a painter, Sarah, a housewife, Elenor (sic), a bookkeeper, Alex, a machinist and the younger children are students.

By the 1930 census, both Sarah and Jacob are naturalized citizens. Now they are listed as both age 50 (Jacob gained 12 years in a decade, Sarah an astonishing 14), Al was 23, Louis 18, Shirley 17 and Hyman, 15. Elinor was not listed, because she had married Isadore Axelrod in 1928.

They owned their own home, said to have been literally built by Jacob (who had been a brick layer and was still listed as plasterer) at 837 Park Ave. in the Williamsburg section of Brooklyn. The house was valued at $8,000 at the time and is the same house that both lived in until their deaths.

Jacob was unable to read or write English, but spoke it and Sarah could neither read, write nor speak it according to the census, but Jacob did have business stationery printed which I still have that seems to contradict that. His stationery lists "192_" as the date (so it was good for ten years) and his phone number is Pulaski 1404. He is "Jacob Levitt, Builder and General Contractor, White Wash By Machine, Brick and Cement Work."

HONE PULASKI 1404   BROOKLYN, N. Y. _____192_

M _____

JACOB LEVITT

Builder and General Contractor

WHITE WASH BY MACHINE
BRICK AND CEMENT WORK   837 PARK AVENUE

Jacob Levitt stationery. It survives because Anna Levitt wrote recipes on the backs.

I remember the house as a child and young adult, for after Sarah's death in 1958, Elinor and her husband Isadore moved into it until it was purchased by the City, then demolished to make way for a hospital in the 1960s. 837 Park Ave. was a plain cream-painted brick row house, built to accommodate the owners as well as tenants (my grandparents lived on the second floor). At some point a second wooden two-story house was built in the rear yard for additional renters. There were four apartments in the front house and two in the rear.

My first memories of it in the 1950s, was that the brick house was by that time pretty worn-looking, but the wooden house in back seemed to be in a lot worse shape. Anna described the original house as, "dilapidated" and the rear house as a, "hovel." The basement was altogether scary for a kid. When I accompanied my father down there to fix something, part of it had no electricity and the ceiling became so low that Louis had to bend down to get to the bricked over boiler.

The neighborhood by then had transitioned from working class to poor. Sarah, widowed since 1950, lived alone. She spoke no English, but was pretty tough and never seemed to worry about the high crime rate in the neighborhood. Today, Williamsburg is the most gentrified neighborhood in Brooklyn, home to artists (most of whom have been outpriced and have left for scruffier neighborhoods where they are outpriced, again), hipsters and Wall Street types. Despite the pleas of her grown children, Sarah stayed in the house.

As a child, the area appeared threatening. Sarah seemed happy to see us when we visited, but did not appear to be a warm person, although she kept a jar of Rice Krispie treats on a high shelf in the kitchen cabinets. There was a skylight in the kitchen and the bathroom toilet had a pull chain from the water tank above to flush it. Since Ira and I did not speak or understand Yiddish, there was little communication between us.

For many American Jewish "Baby Boomers" Yiddish was kept as a secret language by our parents. Anna and Louis spoke it to each other when they didn't want us to know what they were talking about; a similar situation confirmed by most of our friends of the same generation. Also, Yiddish was seen as the dying language of the immigrant generation. It was Old World and post-war American Jews wanted to be part of the New World. I regret not knowing it (although I use many Yiddish expressions in everyday language). I do not, though, know how to speak, read or write it.

Our visits to Sarah as a family were not frequent (Louis went over more often on his own after work), because Anna did not have a good relationship with her mother-in-law. She had told me that Sarah was, "very bossy" and that Jacob was, "a meek man, but a very nice person."

In an email message for this narrative from my cousin Paul Levitt and the oldest member of our generation of Levitt cousins, he wrote, "I'll tell you what Lillian (my Mom) recalled when I spoke to her when she was in her nineties. Unfortunately, that generation was too closed to tell the children much of the past. Our grandparents, I believe came from Russia. Jacob and Sarah came to the U.S. (?) in the early 1900's. Our great grandfather was a fur trapper and was killed by highwaymen when he was returning with a wagon full of furs. Our great grandmother

Jacob Levitt, ca. 1908 in a Jewish New Year card. Why would Jacob send a New Year card without Sarah? A possible reason is that the card was made while he was living as a boarder with a family in Brooklyn, while Sarah was still in Russia. Note spats on shoes. Spats (short for spatter guards, a light-colored cloth accessory) were considered stylish up until the 1920s.

was one of four sisters whose family owned a farm and she might have been the only sister to come to the U.S.

Jacob was a brick layer and did corner work, which made him a specialist. Unfortunately, the Depression did him in and he spent a lot of time making wine for personal consumption in the basement of the small multi-family building they owned, and I suppose they lived on the rents. Essentially, your dad and mine grew up in abject poverty."

The Great Depression lasted from 1929 to 1939 and was the most severe economic downturn in American history.

I remember my parents telling me of seeing blocks-long lines at soup kitchens and people selling apples on street corners. Both Anna and Louis grew up during the Great Depression and like many

Billboard, ca. 1930s

others who lived through those dire times, it had an indelible effect on them. They were thrifty people who could do without. Food was absolutely never wasted; to do so was a sin. Many of Ira and my clothes as youngsters were hand-me-downs from older cousins who had outgrown them. Into old age Anna re-used paper towels, drying them on a rack in the bathtub, when she could have afforded new rolls. My mother-in-law re-used aluminum foil. They never forgot.

I remember asking Anna as a child, why so many of our relatives owned or operated grocery stores and fish markets and she answered that in Europe food was often scarce and if you had a food store here, you knew that no matter how bad business got, you were never going to starve. This specter of hunger followed us even into the Fifties and like so many of my generation, we were chastised to eat everything on our plates, because, "People are starving in Europe." That assertion was never open to debate.

Louis attended PS 148 through 8th grade (graduating in 1925 at age 13). I have two of his autograph albums from that era, one inscribed by him:

In 1929 he graduated from Boys High School and wanted to go to college. He was the most academic and religious of his siblings and the only boy to continue his Jewish studies after his Bar Mitzvah. His parents objected. They wanted him to work, but he enrolled at City University's Brooklyn campus, going to school at night and working during the day. He did that for nine years. During the depth of the Depression, he left college to help support the family. Anna noted, "that he didn't have too much time until he was to get his degree." I always felt that he would have finished his degree after retirement, but he died before he could retire.

Go little album far and near,
Tell all my friends who love me dear,
And make them all to sign a page,
That I may read in my old age.
By Louis Levitt

Neither Anna (as the reader will soon discover) nor her sister-in-law Lillian painted a rosy picture of their in-laws. I did not know my grandfather at all, and my grandmother not that well. Hard times sometimes hardened people.

98

The Levitt Siblings

Left: Elinor and Isadore Axelrod.
Right: Elinor Levitt Axelrod, Sarah Levitt, Shirley Levitt Davis, ca. 1935

Left: Alex Levitt. Right: Hyman Levitt, ca. 1935

Left: Sarah and Jacob Levitt.
Right. Louis Levitt, Atlantic City Boardwalk, ca. 1935

Elinor (born Elke in Yiddish, ca.1905-1987) was the oldest of the Levitt children, born in Vitebsk. Her birth date fluctuated throughout her life; making herself older so she could get working papers as a youth, making herself younger as she aged, and finally trying to prove her original age (she did not have a birth certificate from Vitebsk) when she went to file for Social Security. She was fashionable, common sensical and good with figures, but very careful with money. She generally worked in the clerical and bookkeeping fields throughout her life, but in another era, easily could have been the boss.

Elinor's decision to marry Isadore Axelrod was the sharpest decision of her life, for he worshipped her, worried about her and catered to her. He was a democratic Socialist politically and an all-around good guy, personally. They married in 1928.

Isadore (1895-1988) was also an immigrant, eleven years older than Elinor, arriving in this country from "Russia/Poland" according to the 1920 US Census, in 1907. At age 12, speaking no English, his elementary school principal immediately placed him in either a kindergarten or first grade class, where Isadore towered above his classmates. That was enough of an incentive for him, so he learned English quickly and jumped into an age appropriate grade level.

"Portrait Multiple de Marcel Duchamp" (1917), by Marcel Duchamp, a founder of the Surrealist movement in art. "Duchamp," according to the National Portrait Gallery in Washington, DC, created a, "mechanically produced photo-postcard that depicted him simultaneously from five different vantage points, thanks to a hinged mirror."

Isadore Axelrod, a photographer, recreated the technique in this ca. late 1930s photograph of Elinor.

At age 25, he was living with his parents Jack and Jennie on Simpson St. in the Bronx and was employed as a salesman in silks. In the 1930 US Census, he is listed as a "commercial traveler" (traveling salesman) in the dry goods trade. By then, he and his wife Elinor were living at 158 Quantico Ave. in Baltimore, MD.

Hand-cut silhouette with fabric curtain frame of Elinor and Isadore Axelrod, Atlantic City, ca. 1930s

Once, when going to see clients in the racially segregated Maryland of the early 1930s, he and his assistant, an African-American man had to stay overnight in a small town. They stopped at a number of hotels and motels, but while the managers were willing to put Isadore up for the night, they were unwilling to let his assistant stay in their establishments. Isadore refused at each stop, finally deciding that they would sleep in the car, instead.

In the late 1930s, Isadore and Elinor settled in the beach and boardwalk town of Atlantic City, NJ, living on Pacific Ave. During World War ll, the many large hotels that lined the boardwalk were commissioned by the Armed Forces to house wounded and battle-weary troops for rest and rehabilitation. The hotels were fully occupied and the beach and boardwalk crowded with soldiers and sailors from all over the country. Elinor saw an opportunity to make money and decided that they would open a boardwalk photo studio, with Isadore as the photographer and she doing the business side. It was a huge success. GIs wanted a photo of themselves to send to their parents, wives or girlfriends. My father said that at day's end, they would literally carry cash back to their apartment in their aprons. They were so successful that after the war, Isadore never had to work again, although Elinor continued her office career.

Isadore was a wonderful uncle, caring and with a whimsical sense of humor. When Elinor and he would come to dinners or our seders, they would always bring a box of Barton's candy.

When we would unwrap the box and open it, there were always one or two candies missing. Isadore insisted that he had had to sample the candies to make sure they weren't spoiled. I think he really believed that.

After Sarah Levitt died they moved back to Brooklyn and into 837 Park Ave., buying the siblings' shares of the house and hoping that the City would soon pay more for the property than it was worth, as part of large scale urban renewal in the area. That didn't work out as planned and they lived in that high crime area for several more years until finally, the house was purchased and demolished. They then moved into an apartment in Brighton Beach, Brooklyn, a few blocks from their beloved ocean.

Isadore and Elinor Axelrod. Original graphite sketches signed Greenway, Atlantic City, 8/2/46

As Isadore aged and needed assistance, Elinor was there for him. They could not have children, but they had each other. Elinor died suddenly of a cerebral hemorrhage in her early 80s and at the instant Isadore realized she was gone, he went into a coma-like state that he never recovered from. My brother Ira visited him frequently in the nursing home, but he was never responsive. He could not accept life without, "his girl," as he had always called Elinor. Anna said, "Isadore was a darling man. He was so concerned about everyone. From the day they got married to the day she died, they were lovers."

Elinor and Alex Levitt, ca. 1910, shortly after arriving in America. Photo by A. Warshaw Studio, at 23 Manhattan Ave. and 349 Tompkins Ave. in Brooklyn

The next oldest of Louis's siblings was Alex, who had been born in Belarus, ca. 1907. Alex is listed in the French pages of mother Sarah's (Sora Liba) passport as Elie, a Hebrew name, but his Yiddish name appears to have been Elvel, an uncommon name, according to one translator. Apparently, Alex was a popular name given by Russian immigrants to replace Jewish names from the Old Country. Alex had left school in the eighth grade to help support his family. Just before World War ll, his mother Sarah and older sister Elinor loaned Alex, Louis and Hyman money to purchase the Collins Rapid Laundry and a satellite store that did dry cleaning in the neighborhood of Flushing, in Queens, NY. An elaborate shareholder's certificate dated April 13, 1938 lists Alex Levitt as the president and Louis Levitt as the secretary of the corporation. Paul Levitt (Alex's son) recalls that it lasted eleven years and then it was sold.

He continues: "Alex (his father) told me, one day Frank Costello of

Collins Rapid Laundry 100 shares certificate, dated April 13, 1938. Alex Levitt is listed as President and Louis Levitt, as Secretary

Murder Inc. came by and demanded that they do the laundry work for the hotels he was involved with. Alex told him they were at capacity doing government work for the military. Costello backed off."

Frank Costello rose through the ranks of the Mafia to eventually become the leader of the Luciano (later Genovese) crime family. A skilled operative, he became known as, "The Prime Minister of the Underworld." Throughout his long and bloody career, he associated with many of the pre-eminent stars of the gang world: Lucky Luciano, Bugsy Siegel, Legs Diamond, Mad Dog Coll and many others with equally ruthless power, but less colorful names. Costello was particularly adept at increasing Mafia revenue through the expansion of slot machines and the supervision of "white collar crimes" (gambling, loansharking, etc.) and numerous "legitimate" businesses (maybe he had an eye on the laundry business). Talk about "money laundering"!

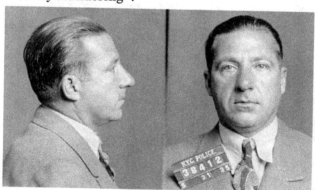

Frank Costello Mug Shot

Paul Levitt continues his family's story: "He and Lillian started a business owning and servicing washing machines (after the Collins Laundry was sold) in the basements of apartment buildings. This resulted in their getting into the middle class. Alex died young at 56, but Lillian was almost 97."

I remember Alex, Lillian and their children Paul and Renie very well. They lived in a leafy, suburban-style neighborhood in Queens when I was growing up, opposite a large church. They were gracious hosts and when Anna had one of several surgeries when we were young, Ira stayed with them and was well taken care of. Alex was very handy and took care of the maintenance of the laundry machines and Lillian handled the books. After the war, many families moved into postwar midrise brick apartment buildings in developing areas of Queens and Long Island. None of those apartments had individual laundry machines, but their building basements were filled with coin-operated washers and dryers. Alex and Lillian created a successful business.

After Alex's death, Lillian, Paul and his wife Leslie and Renie and her husband Arthur Bailyn (later divorced) moved to California. Paul became a prominent surgeon in Beverly Hills (now retired) and Renie recently retired as a psychotherapist.

From left, seated: Renie Levitt Bailyn, Lillian Levitt, Anna Levitt, Louis Levitt, Joel Levitt, Ira Levitt. From Left, standing: Arthur Bailyn, Leslie Levitt, Paul Levitt, Elinor Axelrod, Isadore Axelrod, ca. 1960s

Shirley was the youngest sister. I did not know her well, because some time after her marriage to Sheppard (Shep) Davis, they moved their family (daughter Jacqueline and son Charles) to Paterson, New Jersey and after that, southeast Florida. As a small child, I remember visiting them in NJ and it seemed like they lived in the middle of nowhere. Of course, when you're a small child, every place outside of Brooklyn seems like the middle of nowhere (even as an adult, that still seems somewhat true). In a unique set of circumstances, Shirley and her brother Hyman, married Shep and his sister, Anna Mollie (although not at the same time).

Shirley (1913-1981) was often unwell and eventually lost a leg to diabetes. Shep (1907-1989) was named my godfather (not common in Jewish families, I gather) in part Anna said, because he had stood up for them when they had their troubles with Sarah Levitt (Anna's niece Ethel was my godmother).

Their move to start over in the Miami area, was fortuitous. Southeast Florida was booming in the late fifties and sixties with construction in homes and office buildings. Shep decided to open an office cleaning business and it clicked. The Davises soon purchased a house in Miami. When Charles finished school, he joined Shep in the business. The last time I saw Shep was in 1962, when he came up for my Bar Mitzvah, which Shep felt as my godfather, a responsibility to attend (Shirley was unable to travel). I remember that he had supper with us and he was loud and opinionated, funny and frank. I liked that.

The Davis Family: Sheppard, Charles, Shirley (Levitt), Jacqueline, ca. late 1960s

Shirley and Shep's descendants all live in Florida, I recently was able to reconnect with their daughter Jacqueline (Jacci) Rosenthal Schwartz, after an absence of 60 years and we had a wonderful conversation catching up and going over old times.

Jacci recalled that her father was very active in the local Masonic Temple, which often sponsored dances. Her mother, although she had a prosthetic leg (and these devices were not very sophisticated in those days) was determined to dance with her husband, which she often did.

The youngest Levitt sibling was Hyman (1914-1994). Some time after the Collins Rapid Laundry was sold, Hy entered the Post Office and remained there until his retirement. When Louis was nearing 50 and felt he would not be able to continue the heavy workload and long hours managing the Clover Laundry, Hy encouraged him to take the Post Office exam, which he did.

Hy and Anna Mollie lived in an apartment in Queens, where they raised their sons Charles (Chucky) and Michael (Mickey). Ira and I vividly recall visiting them there when we were young children (they were several years older). They were adamant about not sharing their toys with us (funny, how you never forget stuff like that). As adults, though, they were much friendlier.

Anne Sterman Levitt and Hy Levitt

Anna Mollie and Hy were married several decades, but eventually they divorced and Hy married Anne Sterman. They had a son David and lived in Queens until Hy's death. Anne is my only living aunt on both sides of the family.

David has a daughter Lauren,

who we are proud to say, is currently serving in the US Marine Corps, stationed in Okinawa, Her cousin Jacob Schrift, we are proud to add, has also joined the Marines.

Left: Anne and Hy's granddaughter Lauren Levitt.
Right: Anna Mollie and Hy's great grandson Jacob Schrift

Several years after Hy's death, Anne married Gary Kroll and moved to Amityville, Long Island. We have remained close over the years and are frequently in touch.

The Levitt family in America is now up to our fifth generation.

As Close as Relatives

If you're lucky in life, sometimes you develop friendships that are as strong (if not stronger) than family. Such were the Beckers.

One day in the 1920s when Anna was taking the subway to high school, she noticed a young woman about her age, sitting alone. She went over to her and began a conversation, which began a friendship that lasted three generations. Her name was Ida Becker, and she had a pronounced and disfiguring hunchback.

Hunchback (kyphosis) is rare to see today due to preventative care and advanced surgical treatments, but in those days and throughout my childhood, it was unusual, but not unheard of to see people with such a severe condition. As Anna and Ida became close friends, she learned that Ida's mother Rose worked in a fish market just a few blocks away from where Anna's mother Tillie worked in another fish market. The older women became fast friends, too.

Left: Anna Kaplan and Ida Becker, ca. 1930s. Right: Rose Becker, ca. 1970s

Rose and her husband Joseph were also immigrants from Russia, the former, according to the 1920 US Census arriving here in 1912 and the latter in 1905. Rose had been born ca. 1892 and Joseph, ca. 1885. Joseph worked in a grocery store, but I understand was plagued by ill health and died long before I was born. Rose became the wage earner in the family. They had two

110

children, both born in Brooklyn; Ida in 1914 and Isadore (Izzy) born in 1919.

I recall Ida as warm, but shy and once danced with her at a family celebration when I was probably around eight. She had chronic health issues and must've died in the late 1950s. Mrs. Becker and Izzy became my family's closest friends over the years.

Izzy Becker and his widowed mother Rose, were frequent visitors and favorites of ours. Mrs. Becker was a short, round, older woman with an impish glint in her eyes, magnified by thick glasses. She had had a hard life (a widow, a disabled daughter who had died young, a job like Tillie's in a tough, dirty field), but she also had a zest for life. If Ira or I were sick, she would always visit and bring us a toy: never socks or underwear or something utilitarian. Always a toy, thank God.

Years later, as an art major in college, my portfolio was filled with life drawings of nudes. Mrs. Becker, now elderly, had known me my entire life and was interested in seeing my artwork. I proudly showed her my drawings and she was a bit shocked. "Oy," she exclaimed, "Naketeh maydeles!" (naked girls). She thought a moment and added, "Yosseleh, if you made those pictures, it's okay."

When Izzy was in his sixties, his mother died. He was a bachelor and had lived with her his entire life. He cried out at the cemetery, "Now, I am an orphan." I've never forgotten that, having lost my last parent when I was in my sixties. It's such a poignant observation, and so very true. No matter what our age when our parents die, we become orphans.

Izzy had told me that he dropped out of high school at an early age, because he had no interest in formal education, yet he was smart and hard working. He was immediately employed in local groceries, working his way up to become produce manager at a Waldbaum's Supermarket and eventually joining corporate headquarters as the executive in charge of produce for the entire chain. Corporate life was not for him, though. He needed to squeeze the cantaloupes, smell the lemons and schmooze and kibitz (socialize and joke with) the customers, so he returned to the field. He was Anna and Louis's closest friend and a thoroughly decent man who always had a sense of joy about him. Ira and I used to argue over who would sit next to him at the dinner table and decades later, our daughters Lia and Jessica would do the same.

From left: Lia Levitt, Izzy Becker, Jessica Levitt, ca. 1990s

The Holocaust & Post-War Period

I am hopeful that future generations will never forget what the Holocaust was, or what genocide is, so I will not offer a textbook definition. To attempt to do so in such a short space, would be to do a terrible injustice to its victims.

I was a Post-War baby, so I do not have any direct knowledge of World War ll and the Holocaust, but in a Jewish neighborhood in Brooklyn like Boro Park, the latter was a deep, dark, silent cloud that never floated away. Anna and Louis rarely referenced it directly. We knew of Survivors in our synagogue and in the community, and my parents would literally whisper to us about those people whose arms bore Nazi-inflicted tattoos. There was such dread, that they could not bear to discuss it.

One can only guess if any of our family who stayed behind in Russia and had survived the pogroms, the pestilence and the Russian Revolution, perished during the Holocaust. The last correspondence from Russia that the Muzykants had sent (or at least was saved) dates to 1938. And the last correspondence to the Levitts from relatives in Russia, ended in 1935. It can be assumed that our family and our family history, was destroyed during the war, if not soon afterwards in Stalinist Russia.

I recall seeing newsreel footage of the liberation of the concentration camps in movie theatres prior to the double feature, and also on television in the mid-Fifties. It was horrifying: numb, emaciated survivors staring blankly at the film cameras; piles of withered corpses waiting to be buried. The knowledge that they were Jews like myself made it even more horrifying.

If there is any shred of hope and humanitarianism in me today, it may very well have its roots in those images of our People.

Occupations and Locations

It's often remarkable to see enormous leaps in education and occupation from the first generation of immigrants (of any ethnicity) to the next one or two. There's a caveat, though, when it comes to women. Expectations for girls were not the same as for boys and opportunities were much more limited for women through much of the 20th Century and even, of course, today. On the male Levitt side, my grandfather Jacob was a bricklayer and in America, a contractor. His formal education must have ended in childhood, back in Belarus. His son Alex, also born in Belarus, but in America by age three, left school after 8th grade to help support the family. He and his wife Lillian's son Paul became a physician and their daughter Renie, a psychotherapist.

My father Louis was the only one of his four siblings to have attended college, but he dropped out during the Great Depression to help support the family. He worked in laundries and then, in the Post Office. He and Anna's sons became a teacher (Ira) and a school district administrator (Joel).

On the Kaplan side, my grandfather Isaac was described as a bookbinder in Belarus, but tailor and then grocer in America. His son Benjamin (Morris), also born in Belarus, had an 8th grade education. He became the owner of a drug store in Hartford, CT. He and his wife Becky's sons became a pharmacist (Alex) and physician (Henry). Morris's older brother Julius, also born in Belarus, also had an 8th grade education. He owned a grocery store and he and his wife Rae's sons became a grocer (Jerry) and a physician (Edward).

The range of Levitt/Kaplan occupations opened up with those born in America, third generation, with many Levitts and Kaplans receiving college educations. The following is an incomplete, but informative list, as I have not been able to reach all of my relatives.

First Generation Levitt
Baker
Bricklayer/Contractor

Second Generation Levitt
Cleaning Service Owner
Laundry Worker/Owner
Office Worker
Photography Business Owner
Postal Worker

Third Generation Levitt
Bookkeeper
Cleaning Service Owner
Financial Services
Physician
Postal Worker
Psychotherapist
Sales Administrator
School District Administrator
Teacher

Fourth Generation Levitt
Chiropractor
Corporate Executive
Electrician
Emergency Medical
  Technician
Finance Manager
Jewelry Maker/Small
  Business Owner
Librarian
Military Service Member
Nurse
Physician
Psychiatrist
Psychologist
Roofer
Teacher
Transit Worker

Fifth Generation Levitt
Military Service Member

First Generation Kaplan
Bookbinder/Grocer/Tailor
Fishmonger

Second Generation Kaplan
Candy Store Worker
Drug Store Owner
Grocery Store Owner
House Painter
Office Worker
Tailor

Third Generation Kaplan
Bookkeeper
College Professor
Lawyer/Public Defender
Office Worker
Pharmacist
Physician
Post Office Worker
School District Administrator
Teacher

Fourth Generation Kaplan
Financial Services
Corporate Executive
Jewelry Maker/Small
  Business Owner
Jewelry Store Owner
Lawyer
Nurse
Physician
Police Officer
Psychologist
Rabbi

Fifth Generation Kaplan
Financial Services
Hospital Administrator
Photographer
Physician

Sixth Generation Kaplan
Law Firm Administrator

I haven't been able to reach all of the descendants of Sarah and Jacob Levitt and Tillie and Isaac Kaplan, but listed below is where the ones I have contacted live.

The Levitt Family, although relatively small, stretches from coast to coast. Today, Levitts live in the following states: NY, CT, PA, FL, IL, MT, NV, OR and CA. Only one descendent, Ira Levitt and his family continue to live in Brooklyn.

The Kaplan Family also has a nationwide presence, with family living in NY, NJ, CO, CT, FL, MI, NC, NV, VA, AZ, and TX. Several Kaplan descendants remain in Brooklyn.

Anna & Louis Meet & Marry

*The original silk tie that Louis Levitt wore on the blind date
to meet Anna Kaplan, 1946. Anna and Louis Levitt wedding photo
in original painted glass and porcelain frame, 1947*

The husband of Anna's friend from Lerner's, Adele Wagner had a shoe store that was located next door to the Collins Rapid Laundry, which was owned by Louis Levitt's family in Flushing, Queens. Adele decided to set up Anna and Lou on a blind date and convinced her husband to give Louis, Anna's phone number. Louis called and a date and time were scheduled to meet. They almost didn't make it.

Louis had told her they would meet on a Saturday evening at 8:30pm after he left the laundry, under the clock at Penn Station in Manhattan, a popular and safe meeting place. He said that she'd recognize him in a brown and beige silk tie. By 9:00pm he still had not shown up and Anna said she was, "disgusted." After all, she was in her thirties and one can imagine that she had been stood up before. She resolved to leave and was taking the escalator up to the main floor when she noticed a black-haired man wearing a tie (it was really brown and yellow, not beige) had arrived at the clock. She got off and took the down escalator.

"Are you Lou Levitt?" she asked with annoyance. "Why are you late?"

Louis apologized and said that they had to close the laundry late that night and he had missed the train. That was in June of 1946, when Anna was about to turn 33 and Louis was soon to turn 35.

Just before Anna's birthday on July 5 (Louis's was on July 2), Louis gave Anna a $5 gift certificate to the A.S. Beck Co. shoe store as a birthday present. Later that summer, he took her to Atlantic City to meet his older sister and brother-in-law, Elinor and Isadore Axelrod. It was at that time that Lou proposed to Anna on the Boardwalk. He gave her a ring a few months later, because his family "knew someone in the business."

Anne Kaplan

Louis Levitt

Betrothed

September, Nineteen hundred and forty-six

Left: Engagement announcement. Note: Anna was known as Anne, much of her adult life, but was called Anna again, once she moved to Danbury
Right: Anna and Louis Engagement Weekend, Atlantic City, 1946.
Note: Louis is wearing the same tie he wore when he met Anna on their blind date

Then things got complicated.

Louis had been married previously, also to a woman named Anna. It had been a short and unhappy marriage. Elinor had assured Anna that the first Mrs. Louis Levitt was, "not a nice person and that she had hated Louis and made his life miserable." Divorces at that time were very difficult to obtain and legally acceptable causes for divorce were narrowly defined. In order to obtain one, the first Anna Levitt made up a story that she had caught Louis in, as my mother phrased it, "a compromising position," which Elinor assured her wasn't true. I imagine money had been offered to the first Anna to make this happen. It's probable that Elinor and Isadore had made the payment as they had done extremely well financially during the war. It appears that Elinor had introduced Louis to the first Anna, and that also played into her sense of responsibility for the bad marriage.

My brother Ira and I knew absolutely nothing about our father's first marriage and divorce until months after he died. Our parents had kept it a secret all those years and Anna only reluctantly told us when we went to the local Social Security office to find out about her survivor's benefits. While we waited, our mother tearfully told us the story and how she feared that the first Anna might reappear after all those years to make a claim on her benefits. She was distraught, even though there was absolutely no chance that that would or could happen. Still, we never spoke to her about the subject, again. There's something about sons and a mother's tears that settles all matters.

I think that she kept that secret so that we would not be disappointed in our father, although that would not have happened. He had a great deal of moral rectitude and I think she might have thought his image would be tarnished. Divorce in the 1940s was more than likely thought of as some kind of moral failing. It is hard to believe today that divorces were once so difficult to obtain. Until 1985, the only way to get a divorce in New York State was to prove adultery. Cardinal Spellman, longtime Archbishop of New York, had tremendous moral and political clout and was vigorously opposed to liberalizing civil divorce laws. Folks who could afford it, travelled to Reno, Nevada, which was known as, "The Divorce Capital of the United States" for its open divorce laws and short residency rules for out-of-staters. That was out of the question for Louis, who could neither afford the cost, nor the time off from work.

Anna and Louis Levitt
civil wedding certificate

So, while Anna and Louis's engagement was settled, the path to their wedding was not. They had a civil ceremony in Hoboken, NJ on Dec. 21, 1946, witnessed by Anna's nephew Oscar Bromberg and Louis's brother-in-law Sheppard Davis, probably in case the religious wedding was to fall through. They had had difficulty with Louis's mother (apparently not with his father) over the wedding plans, although the wedding reception and religious ceremony were scheduled a few weeks later on Jan. 12. While the wedding invitation had the usual, "Mrs. Tillie Kaplan, Mr. and Mrs. Jacob Levitt request the honor of your presence....," Anna and Tillie wound up paying for the wedding. Louis had no money of his own and worked for the family laundry and it seems that his mother wouldn't contribute to the wedding costs.

Worse, the evening before the wedding, Anna and Tillie had been "summoned" to Louis's parents' house. His mother Sarah told them that they would not be permitted to go on a honeymoon. None of her other children had gone on honeymoons and the business could not afford for Louis to take time off. According to Anna, Tillie argued in favor of their going, but to no avail. Louis told Anna afterward that they would secretly take a honeymoon weekend in Atlantic City, which they did. Anna said that Louis's father Jacob never said

120

a word throughout the argument. She said he was, "very nice, but meek" and that his wife, "controlled the household."

Of course, Sarah Levitt is not here to present her side of the story, but this is the story as told to me by my mother. Families are complicated. That's for sure.

Anna and Louis Levitt Ketubah (marriage contract)

In the meantime, the ketubah (wedding contract) was signed and the wedding reception apparently went well. It was held at Temple Mason at 1237 Eastern Parkway in Brooklyn on Sunday afternoon at 1pm, Jan. 12, 1947. My parents kept the original bill for 120 guests (coincidentally, exactly the same amount of people Barbara and I had at our wedding in 1973 and our daughter Jessica and son-in-law Joe had at their wedding in 2006) and it came to a total of $405, including food, beverages, tips, hat check and ceremony.

The bridal party consisted of Anna's friend Mae Papier as Maid of Honor and Louis's older brother Al as Best Man. Anna's cousin Abe Constantine (another Musicant

Anna and Louis Levitt wedding invitation

121

musician) led the trio, which consisted of Abe on piano, plus a trumpet player and a sax player.

Anna and Louis Levitt were married for 31 years, until Louis's death in 1978.

Anna & Louis: Early Years, Together

Anna and Louis Levitt established their first home together when Louis moved into the apartment at 4611 10th Avenue in Boro Park that Anna and Tillie shared. The building was a four-family brick house and their place was a three-room apartment, with the Levitts using the bedroom and Tillie sleeping on a fold-out couch in the living room.

Anna and Louis Levitt, ca. 1947. Note the running board on their car, which is either a Hudson or a Plymouth.

Ira (Feb. 2, 1948) and Joel (Feb. 11, 1949), were born while the Levitts lived there, both at Israel Zion Hospital (now Maimonides Medical Center) and both delivered by Dr. Gragutsky.

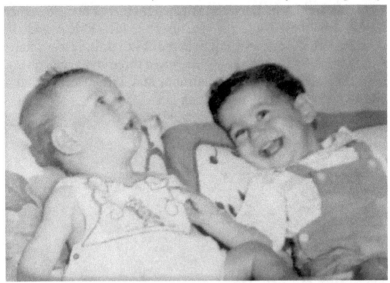

Ira and Joel Levitt, 1949

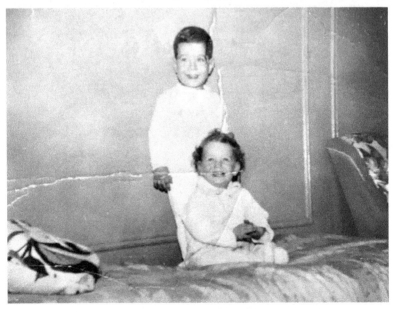

Ira and Joel Levitt, 1950

Ira and Joel Levitt, 1952.

Ira and Joel Levitt, 1953

4303 10th Ave. in 2017. The façade has been completely bricked over and gated and there are security cameras. The grocery was on the first floor and our apartment, on the second. Now it looks like it belongs in a penal colony.

Things soon got cramped after the arrival of us boys, but it wasn't until the early 1950s when all five of us moved into a large three-bedroom apartment above the grocery store owned by Anna's sister Fannie at 4303 10th Avenue. This spacious apartment had five rooms: a master bedroom, a children's bedroom shared by Ira and Joel, a small bedroom for Tillie, a living room with a skylight, an eat-in kitchen, an entry foyer, which contained a dining table pushed against a wall and one bathroom. And it was close to shopping....literally!

For their first anniversary, Louis wanted to purchase a nice piece of furniture for Anna, but lacked the funds. He had been a stamp collector since his teen years, building up a modest collection with his savings. He sold it to buy a mahogany breakfront (now in my home library). It sounds a bit like an O. Henry short story and Anna was truly touched by his sacrifice. Over the ensuing years, he began collecting stamps, again.

Louis was a serious collector hampered by a serious lack of money. He had a keen appreciation of history and geography and concentrated his modest purchases on US postage stamps and first day covers. Over the years he dabbled in selling stamps as a sideline, calling his business the Levitt Stamp Company. He would mail collectors stamps on "approval." They would pay for what they wanted and mail the rest back. Years after he died, we followed his instructions and sold his stamp collection at H.E. Harmer, a Manhattan philatelic auction house he trusted. Barbara, Ira and I attended the auction and we were the only ones there, although a number of lots were offered for sale. It was not like TV auctions: no bidding wars, no excitement. His collection was purchased over the phone.

When the State of Israel came into being in 1948, he collected all stamps Israeli and in appreciation for the heroic actions of the Danish people in saving most of their Jewish citizens from impending death after the Nazi's invaded their country (Danish Jews escaped by boat to Sweden, which was officially neutral during the war), he collected the stamps of Scandinavian countries.

When I was an undergrad at Brooklyn College in the late 1960s, I had an education professor named Prof. Abrahamson, an imperious Dane, who as it turned out was Jewish. He had heard that I was an art major and one day asked me to stay after class. It turned out that he was giving a speech later in the year at Hunter College in commemoration of Denmark's saving of its Jews and later would do the same in Copenhagen. He asked if I could create a calligraphy scroll to bring with him to Denmark and I agreed. Barbara and I attended the program at Hunter as his guests and the scroll was displayed for years at the Museum of the Danish Resistance in Copenhagen. Louis was quite proud.

Left: Louis at the Middle Village, Queen PO, where he worked. Right: Louis at his rotating philatelic history exhibit at the main Flushing, Queens PO

Toward the end of his Post Office career, Louis wrote a philately column for a community newspaper in Queens and mounted photo history exhibits drawn from his collection, at the Flushing Post Office. To this day, Ira collects first day covers and attends the same stamp collecting conventions our father took us to as kids and I am obsessed with maps and geography.

Louis also wrote poetry to Anna, sometimes as greeting cards and often written on scraps of paper. Sadly, none of those exist today.

The heart of the apartment was, of course, the kitchen. Anna finally had room to cook and cook, she did (and she did it quite well). Louis was not a fussy eater, unlike his sons, and ate just about anything, as long as it was kosher. Monday and Thursday suppers were always dairy (noodle kugel, borsht, bananas and sour cream, pot cheese, salad, canned tuna, salmon or sardines in tomato sauce, etc.).

It was in that apartment that I remember starting to draw. Not at a desk (only the kids on the "Ozzie and Harriet" TV show had such a luxury), but sitting on the gray-carpeted floor of the living room, using the scalloped marble top of an ornate coffee table, instead. My father used to bring home the cardboard backing that kept pressed shirts stiff (the Collins Rapid Laundry folded years ago and he now worked as the manager of Clover Laundry and Dry Cleaning) and I drew on the shiny white sides. I wish I had some of those drawings that I still have stored in my memory.

My parents recognized my artistic ability and the fact that there were few opportunities for expressing it in school. There were no elementary school art teachers in those days. We took turns painting at an easel in our classrooms at PS 131 and the wait could take weeks. We had a neighbor whose son was an art student at Pratt Institute in the downtown neighborhood of Ft. Greene. Pratt was a famous art and engineering college and this young man took me to children's art classes by subway every Saturday morning for a period of time. I remember that we made a papier mache piñata one day, smashing it gleefully until the candies poured out. I really appreciate my parents' foresight in making those arrangements.

This young man (I wish I could remember his name) had a girlfriend who attended a small Catholic college, also downtown. One day, he took me to her dormitory to pick her up. Situations like that were taken very seriously in those days. It was a women's dorm and the matron eyed us suspiciously. He had to sign in and was grilled like he was taking a prison inmate out on furlough. We had to wait for her to meet us in the lobby, as males were not permitted upstairs.

Boro Park in the '50s was a largely insular community of immigrants and first-generation strivers; heavily Jewish and Italian. As a kid, no one I knew had a grandparent who spoke English well, no matter what their ethnicity. Middle aged and elderly Italian widows dressed in black from head to toe regardless of how long ago their husbands had died. The teenage Italian boys looked like they were extras in a production of "West Side Story." Our friends around the corner were named Dominic and Junior (the latter being more of a status than a name, for we never learned what his given name really was).

The Jewish community was Orthodox, but not ultra-Orthodox and Chassidic as it is today. Social life often revolved around Torah Moshe, the impressive and ornate Moorish-style synagogue across the street that we saw daily from our living room windows. Louis became the president of the Men's Club. Morris Goldstein, the synagogue president was the brother-in-law of Anna's niece Ethel's husband, Lou Golden. He was a dapper elderly immigrant who owned a men's haberdashery

Torah Moshe synagogue, 10th Ave. & 43rd St. Boro Park; now a girls' yeshiva

in the City. The Recording Secretary was good family friend Nat Honig, whose wife Sylvia was a good friend of Anna's. Their son

Ronnie was one of our friends (after about 45 years, I reconnected with him. He and his family now live in a Dallas suburb).

The rabbi was an eloquent English-speaking scion of a distinguished family of Torah scholars, Chaim Twersky. Rabbi Twersky was known as a brilliant, opinionated man with no

small ego. He had been adopted as a small child into the Twersky clan. He liked to tell the story about being on a flight and seated next to two non-Jewish young women. The rabbi, dressed in black suit and black hat with a beard to match was the object of their curiosity and they asked him why he was dressed like that. That set off a flight's worth of explanations about Judaism that he said the young women were eager to hear. They had many questions and the flight went quickly.

Tillie Kaplan seated on park bench,
ca. early 1950s

Someone in the synagogue asked the rabbi if he in turn, asked the women any questions about their religion, given that they were willing to learn about his.

"Who's interested in their religion!," he declared. And that, ended that.

There was playground down the block that was all concrete with a ribbon of grass surrounding it and scattered park benches. Tillie used to camp out there with her friends, often discussing the latest news in the famed Yiddish-language newspaper, "Forvitz" ("Forward"). Tillie was proud that she could read English, but the "Forvitz" was the newspaper of the working classes and had a strong history in helping to acculturate immigrant Jews. Decades later the newspaper tried out an English language insert (it now has a separate monthly English magazine), as speaking Yiddish was dying out. In the 1980s, I had written an article about the annual Yiddish festival (no longer celebrated) at Lake Waubeeka, a lakefront Danbury community. It had been founded after the war by Jewish NYC firefighters, when Jews were discriminated against in purchasing homes in the private waterfront developments that dotted Candlewood Lake. The article was reprinted in the "Forvitz" English insert and I could only imagine how Tillie would have "kvelled" (burst with pride) if she had lived long enough to share her grandson's "Forvitz" article with her park bench cronies.

My article, "Yiddish Night and Yiddishkeit" appeared in the English insert of this edition of the "Forward," Sept. 7, 1983

My grandmother died in 1956. She had had a hard life: widowed with a young son at an early age, emigrating with him to a strange new land, learning to speak and read English, taking on a new family, widowed again in 1931, working as a fishmonger, no doubt a dirty and smelly occupation, dealing with a heart condition and near blindness, but my recollection of her is of a strong, determined woman; affectionate and with a warm smile. You didn't cross her, though. When I was about five I picked up a curse word at the local playground and repeated it at home, even though I had no idea of its meaning. Tillie wouldn't hear of it. She literally washed my mouth out with soap. Maybe that's why I don't use foul language today.

The Levitts Move to Dahill Road

Anna recalled that in third grade, my teacher told Louis and her that I should take a test to enter the IGC (Intellectually Gifted Children) program that ran in grades four through six at PS 230 in the nearby Kensington section of Brooklyn. She said Louis and she were initially anxious about my taking the 13th Ave. bus alone, but it turned out that there were a few other neighborhood children who made the cut. And so, I did (ironically, when we moved, Ira had to take the bus back to Boro Park to finish up at PS 131).

By that time, the building at 4303 10th Ave. that housed the grocery at store level, a tiny apartment in back and the spacious apartment above that we lived in was sold to the Jarmarks, a family of Jewish refugees who had fled the 1956 Hungarian Revolution. They lived in the truly dark and miniscule back apartment and eventually decided to move upstairs. Ira recalled that they were nice about it and gave us time to find a new place. Since I was already attending PS 230, Anna went apartment hunting in Kensington. She ran into a lot of trouble as no landlord or landlady wanted to rent to a family with two young boys. That is, until she met Mrs. Stern.

Sophie and Harry Stern owned a semi-detached two-story brick house at 154 Dahill Road, just a few blocks from my school. When Anna told Mrs. Stern that there were two boys in our family, she was unfazed. She explained that she had two sons (adults by then) and saw no problem. The problem, though, was with the apartment. The Sterns lived upstairs with Mrs. Stern's widowed sister, Ida McCarthy. The original downstairs apartment had been subdivided years ago into a small one-bedroom apartment, plus. Behind a locked door at the back of this apartment, accessible from a separate side entrance and down a short hallway were two bedrooms, each occupied by bachelors. The problem was we all shared a single hallway bathroom. Anna was appalled, but she had no other place to move us and the new school year was approaching. Mrs. Stern sympathized and said we should not live in a place we were not comfortable in and therefore, she would not insist on our signing a lease. We never did have a lease and we lived there about 16 years.

Left: Ida McCarthy   Center: Sophie Stern   Right: Harry Stern

The rent was initially $75 a month. The Sterns never raised it in all the time we lived there. Instead, every few years Anna and Louis raised their own rent, slipping extra cash into an envelope. Neither the Levitts nor the Sterns ever acknowledged the difference. The apartment was cramped, though. Anna and Louis had the sole bedroom and Ira and I shared the living room, sleeping on uncomfortable "Danish Modern" couches on opposite sides of the small room. The bathroom situation remained an embarrassment for Anna as long as we lived there. Both bachelors worked days and ate all of their meals out, so we rarely saw them. Mr. Zuckerberg was an older man and Mr. Levy, middle-aged. He was educated, extremely shy and with a pronounced stutter. Neither man, to our knowledge, ever had visitors, although the former had a niece. When Mr. Levy was ill with pneumonia, Anna took care of him. After he recovered he gave her a watch in gratitude.

The Sterns and Mrs. McCarthy (whom we called, "Aunt Ida") were wonderful people and we became part of their extended family. Although Anna and Sophie became close friends, they always referred to each other as, "Mrs. Stern" and Mrs. Levitt." Virtually every night, Anna went upstairs to visit with the Sterns and Aunt Ida.

Harry was the business agent for the supermarket workers' union, an important position. He seemed to know everyone in the grocery trade and arranged for Louis to add a sixth day of work to his postal clerk job: Saturdays behind the cheese counter in a supermarket in Queens. When Ira came of age, Mr. Stern got him a job at a Big Apple supermarket in Brooklyn. Ida worked in an office at A&S (Abraham and Strauss), a classic downtown Brooklyn department store, while Sophie, like Anna was a "housewife."

Harry was a large man with a large personality. He was very generous, giving Ira and me tickets he had received to the World Series when the Yankees made repeat appearances in the 1960s. Somehow, I have always been an avid St. Louis Cardinals fan, although I don't know why (red is not my favorite color; purple is). From 1960 to 1964 the Yankees played in five consecutive World Series. In 1964, the Cardinals beat them in seven games. I was thrilled and got to see all of the Cardinal greats: Ken Boyer, Curt Flood, Bill White, Julian Javier, the incredible Bob Gibson and Lou Brock (I saw the great Stan Musial, Hall of Famer and recipient of the Presidential Medal of Freedom play in his final year when he appeared against the Mets), as well as Maris, Mantle, Berra, etc. from the Yankees.

Many years later I met Lou Brock outside the Baseball Hall of Fame in Cooperstown, NY. At a table set up on the sidewalk on my side of the street sat the infamous Reds star Pete Rose, a large crowd clamoring to meet him and purchase an autograph. Across the street was a similar table with absolutely no one standing in line. I recognized Lou Brock sitting there. I rushed across the street and like a star-struck fan blurted out, "Mr. Brock, I've been a Cardinals fan my whole life, ever since

St. Louis Cardinals Hall of Famer Lou Brock's autograph on my Baseball Hall of Fame program

I was a small child in Brooklyn, which got me beat up a lot (not entirely true). He was so gracious. His wife wanted to charge me for his autograph (which was fine with me), but he interceded. "No charge," he told her. "He's a Cardinals fan from Brooklyn!"

After Harry Stern died of a heart attack, Louis became the only driver among the families and took Sophie, Ida and Anna on errands and to doctor's appointments. Sophie, like Harry, was a large person with health problems, so she always sat in the front passenger seat. Decades later, the Stern grandchildren (Alan, Fran and Hallie), whom I knew as children, found me on Facebook and the two sisters came to Anna's unveiling in Long Island (near where all three siblings live). We had quite a reunion.

Life on Dahill Road was excellent. On the other side of the semi-detached house was a family named Gales, whose daughter Linda and I reconnected with recently on Facebook. Across the common driveway on the other side was a similar semi-detached two-story that housed three generations of the DeSalvo/DiSalvo and Matrisciani families. Collectively, they were terrific neighbors. Anna had said, "We lived next door to an Italian family. They were wonderful neighbors. Those were happy years"

*Dahill Rd, from left: The Gales at corner (bottom floor); the Sterns (top floor)
and Levitts (bottom floor) at No. 154 (it was not obscured by foliage at the time);
the DeSalvos across driveway; the Matriscianis (bottom floor)
and the DiSalvos (top floor)*

In warm weather, the neighbors; children and adults alike and Ira and I played slapball (a baseball-like game where you hit a pink "Spaldeen" with the open palm of your hand) in the shared concrete backyard. Louis never joined us, as he was older, not interested in sports and tired from a long day's work. Sal DiSalvo and Danny Matrisciani played too, and acted as coaches. Mary Jane DeSalvo, Elaine DiSalvo and Gilda Matrisciani cheered us on. It was the only "organized" sport Ira and I regularly played and added tremendously to our childhoods. Elaine and Sal's older daughter DyAnne DiSalvo, is now a noted children's book author and illustrator.

PS 230 was a more "modern" school than the one I had left in Boro Park and the IGC classes were largely composed of bright, competitive kids. My fourth-grade teacher, a wise and tough-love practitioner named Mrs. Beckinella, advised Anna and Louis at a parent-teacher conference that I would benefit by being given more responsibility. My parents assigned me to garbage duty at home; a task I have never been able to shake. In fifth grade, I had Mrs. Rose Cohn, a tall distinguished woman who later became the school's principal. My sixth-grade teacher was a young red-haired man. Today, he would be labelled a sexual predator, for he paid the girls an unnatural amount of attention and encouraged them to sit on his lap. At the time, we did not process his behavior as such; the boys in class just being annoyed that the girls got preferential treatment. How sickeningly naïve.

At PS 230 I made three lifelong friends, Ronald Prishivalko and his older sister Geraldine and Marshall Adesman. Gerry still lives in Brooklyn, but Ron and his family live in Virginia and Marshall and his wife in Tennessee. We still keep in touch.

I lived at 154 and continued to sleep on my foam slab couch until I married Barbara Robinson in 1973. Our first apartment together was a few blocks away in a low-rise apartment building at 36 Dahill Road. Even though Ira now had the living room all to himself, about a year later Anna, Louis and Ira moved to a spacious two-bedroom apartment in Bay Ridge, about ten blocks from Barbara's parents, Kay and Harry Robinson, which he lived in until he got married in 1977 to Barbara Harfosh.

Ira had met Barbara H. in 1973, when she was a substitute teacher at PS 94 in the Sunset Park neighborhood of Brooklyn, where he spent his entire teaching career. They didn't date, though, until two years later. Barbara went on to a successful career in a major insurance company, becoming a vice president. A music major in college, she also performed as a member of the chorus of The Bronx Opera. They have a wonderful son, Joshua Michael and now a lovely daughter-in-law, Melissa.

Left: Barbara Harfosh and Ira Levitt, 1978.
Right: Melissa and Joshua Levitt, 2018

Summers

As a very young child, I remember Louis carrying me on his shoulders into the cooling waters of Coney Island beach, although I don't recall being thrilled with my high perch. Coney Island has a long and rich history as the "Poor People's Riviera" and the home of Nathan's annual hot dog eating contest. The 2018 winner, Joey Chestnut broke his own record by eating 74 hot dogs and buns in 10 minutes. Yech!

Louis at Coney Island. Note: Parachute Jump ("The Eifel Tower of Brooklyn") in background, ca. 1949. The original Nathan's of Coney Island. Bottom row from left: Briella Bittner, Joey Bittner, Haley Bittner, Ira Levitt. Top row from left: Jessica Bittner, Joseph Bittner, Melissa Wu, Barbara Levitt, 2017

Ira and I have vague memories of the first place in "The Country" when our family vacationed there in the early fifties. That was Morristown, NJ, where I remember being chased by an irate swan at a lakefront park. Photos indicate that we stayed in rooms at a large rooming-type house and that it was a happy time for all of us.

More vivid memories are of Rockaway Beach in Queens, where like many striving postwar families we rented rooms (kitchen with couch and a single bedroom with two double beds) in an aged, sprawling house that had been converted into summer rental apartments. It was little kid heaven as we were down the block from the oceanfront beach and there were loads of similar age children to play with. At the end of each summer season, the families in the boarding houses that lined the street threw a big block party for everyone. The highlight was always a mock wedding, featuring a burly guy dressed in drag as the bride. Louis, as one of the more observant folks on the block, always played the role of the rabbi who married the couple.

After we moved to Dahill Road we spent summers in the tiny Catskills hamlet of White Lake, a village within the town of Bethel, where the Woodstock festival took place in 1969 at the dairy farm of Max Yasgur (Anna remembered seeing "hippies" swimming nude in the lake). So, the closest any of the Levitts got to the "Summer of Love" was Anna (by then, I was working summers as an elevator operator and Ira, at the Raleigh Hotel).

The Sterns spent summers nearby at Fialkoff's, a massive bungalow colony in the epicenter of Borsht Belt Jewish life; the rural "metropolis" of Monticello. Fialkoff's was pretty upscale, with a large "Casino"; a nongambling building (other than poker and mah jong) where there were weekend shows featuring comedians and song acts. We would visit them, occasionally.

Our place was much more modest. Laurel House was owned by Thelma and Sol (Samuel) Mondlin, an older couple who rented rooms in a creaking farmhouse and a scattering of bungalows across the road from beautiful White Lake, with additional waterfront property. Our bungalow consisted of an eat-in screened porch with a great view of the lake, a small kitchen and two small bedrooms. Our lives were spent outdoors; picking wild berries up on the hills above our bungalow, fishing and catching crawdads, swimming and rowing at the lake and running around with the children of families like ours, who rented the same places year after year. It was idyllic.

White Lake, NY. Top photo left: View of White Lake from the crest of the hill behind our bungalow. Top photo right: Anna holding one of the house kittens, whom we named, Gertrude C. Katz. Bottom left photo: The Levitts, relaxed. Bottom photo right: Barbara Robinson and Joel Levitt. All photos date from 8/69

The Mondlins themselves, were a unique couple. He was kindly, forever busy trying to sustain the life of a ramshackle farmhouse that seemingly wished to be put out of its misery. Thelma was the business person, but they both were devotees of a philosophy called Aesthetic Realism. They had the only television on the property, and in order to watch it, you sometimes had to hear a spiel about Aesthetic Realism first. I doubt any of us understood it and certainly, no one embraced it, but the lure of watching Jackie Gleason in, "The Honeymooners" was too strong to resist.

141

Anna and Louis on steps of our Laurel House bungalow, 1969

The Mondlins had a modest wooden building on site which they maintained as a summer theatre. They were interested in the Arts and rented it out to young performers from Manhattan, where they lived in the off-season. The actors and actresses at the White Lake Playhouse stayed in the dormered rooms in the farmhouse attic and put on cabaret-style shows, as well as a few musicals. The theatre had a small stage and folding chairs for the audience. It always lost money, but the Mondlins persevered. They were a very nice couple who had a son who for many years was a manager of the humongous Strand Book Store in the City, a NYC landmark. I remember seeing him on one of my many visits to the store as a young adult and mentioning his parents to him, fondly, but he was pretty gruff. Maybe he had heard one too many lectures on Aesthetic Realism.

It was at White Lake that I had my first romantic kiss. She was a local girl (and therefore not Jewish), maybe a year or two older than my twelve or thirteen years, slender, with long black hair and eyes heavily lined in black. I do not recall her name, but I do recall the kiss. Sorry Barbara.

In later years when we were dating, Barbara would spend some weekends at White Lake. To maintain modesty, she had to sleep in my parents' double bed with Anna, while Louis slept in one of the single beds in the other bedroom (I had the other). By that time, Ira was working summers and staying at the Raleigh Hotel in nearby South Fallsburg.

Louis, like all the working husbands in "The Country" worked weekdays back in Queens and only came up on weekends, except for his two-week vacation. The roads (there was no Interstate in those days) were clogged by these Catskills commuters on Friday evenings. On Sunday evenings Louis schlepped back to Brooklyn laden with a week's worth of cooked dinners tightly wrapped in aluminum foil (he didn't know how to cook), his Chevrolet Biscayne groaning under the accumulated weight and cholesterol of soups, potted meats and roast chicken. He only drove American cars. Chevy's he firmly stated; never Fords, because Henry Ford, the founder of Ford Motor Co. and a titan of American industry, was a notorious anti-Semite.

The Catskills have been in economic decline for decades and the beginning of the end began when air travel became more desirable and financially feasible for Jewish families. Today, the hotels are gone, but at one time the area was aglow with big name establishments like Grossinger's, the Concord, Kutscher's, Brown's and dozens and dozens of small hotels and bungalow colonies. What is left of the latter are now ultra-Orthodox and Chassidic. To lift the decades-long economic malaise, a new billion-dollar gambling casino, hotel and recreational facility has been built on the site of the old Concord Hotel.

In its heyday, though, "The Mountains" glittered. Many major comedians and singers of the mid-20th century got their starts there, often as "tummlers"; paid extroverts who entertained guests at the pool and in the hotel lobbies. The idea was to give the customers more attention, food and activities than they would ever need. In enormous dining halls, waiters would bring multiple entrees and desserts to individual guests, without even asking. Excess was the word of the day. To a large degree, the cult film, "Dirty Dancing" got it right

The bungalow colonies, though, were do-it-yourself. You did your own cooking and cleaning. If you weren't on a lake, there was a swimming pool. In the smaller places, you made your own entertainment, gathering with neighbors in the evenings to talk, talk, talk until the mosquitoes drove you inside.

The Catskills were an important and formative force in the acculturation of Jews into American life. The hotels were kosher, which was a necessity for the older generations, but less and less important for younger suburban Jews. In the 1930s, 40s & 50s Jews were still being discriminated against in housing and employment and felt safer and more relaxed among their own people. For children who suffered during the Great Depression, excess was a luxury they could now afford and felt comforted by during the post-war period. With the exception of Ira, who worked at the Raleigh, the Levitts rarely stayed at the hotels; only late in life, when changing over the dishes, etc. became difficult for them, did Anna and Louis spend a few Passovers at the Raleigh when Ira was able to get them a discount. Mostly, our summer lives were lived in the bungalows...and we loved it.

INDOOR "POMPEII POOL" AT THE RALEIGH HOTEL

Adolescence and Older

Ira Levitt Bar Mitzvah, 1961

Ira had his Bar Mitzvah in 1961 and I followed a year later. Both were held at the Torah Moshe synagogue in Boro Park. The receptions were held in the same catering hall, as well; the Little Temple Beth Jacob on Buffalo Ave., off Eastern Pkwy. We also had the same band: "Presenting the Voice and Electronic Accordion of Roy Siegel and his Orchestra." And we studied with the same teacher, a venerable old man, "Rabbi" Schonberg, at his home in Boro Park, which we walked to from Kensington. He really drilled us on our Hebrew and Haftorah lessons and when we said we didn't know something, he would rasp agitatedly, "You don't know! You don't begin to know!" At that point his middle-aged daughter would come into the kitchen to calm him down. In spite of his impatience, we actually liked the old man and we did fine on our Bar Mitzvah days, which made him proud and relieved (he didn't attend, as he could not walk that far and did not ride on the Sabbath).

Since my Bar Mitzvah was slated for January, not my birthday month of February (the Hebrew calendar is lunar-based), but either month would be cold, Anna and Louis said I needed a black wool suit. Someone in the family knew someone in the business and we went to a men's store on Pitkin Avenue under the El (elevated subway line). It was the first time I had my in-seam measured and I thought to myself, "Now, this is weird." In those days there were no soft, lightweight, breathable wool fabrics and I wound up with an incredibly itchy heavy

Joel Levitt Bar Mitzvah, 1962

wool garment (it must have been manufactured during the Inquisition). I whined and whined and my parents came up with a solution. I wore my pajama bottoms under the pants at my Bar Mitzvah.

At that time and in that synagogue, the Bar Mitzvah boy was not the star of any particular Shabbos (Sabbath) service, only a supporting actor with a very limited role. At the appropriate time I was brought up to the bimah (the ornate platform in the center of the synagogue) to chant my Haftorah (a selection from the Prophets) and when it was over I was rewarded with a few shouts of, "Mazel Tov" and my father escorted me back to my seat. My mother, way up in the women's balcony later said that she could barely see or hear me. That was it. Now I was a man.

Bar Mitzvah parties didn't have themes then (Bat Mitzvahs for girls were not introduced until years later). It was customary to receive fountain pens as gifts (writing with a fountain pen is a lost, luxurious art), as well as congratulatory telegrams (generally, receiving a telegram meant some out-of-town relative had died, but not that day).

Anna and Louis were very proud, but life resumed its normal course soon after. Louis had been working six days a week since he had graduated from high school. He was not happy in the Post Office, for he had an unbending work ethic that he did not feel his co-workers shared. He did it to, "make a living," an expression common then, but rarely heard now. He did not have the luxury of having a career or a profession as I did, although he was a smart, honest and hard worker. His role was to provide for his family, and that he did. In his early sixties he suffered a "mild" heart attack and had to cut back by eliminating his Saturday job at the supermarket.

In 1978 at the age of 66 and just months before he planned to retire, my father died of a massive heart attack. He had just finished his breakfast (my mother blamed herself, for insisting that he eat a big breakfast) and collapsed without regaining consciousness. Barbara and I were living in New London, CT at the time and it came as an enormous shock. Rabbi Twersky conducted the funeral. At its conclusion, my mother had a heart attack, right there in the chapel!

That was another shock. We had to immediately decide who would accompany the ambulance with Anna to the hospital and who would accompany the hearse with Louis to Wellwood Cemetery, far out in Long Island. Their dear friend Izzy Becker said he would go to the hospital and Ira's wife Barbara offered to go with him.

Joel, Louis and Ira Levitt, Rockaway Beach, NY, ca. 1955

Barbara, Ira and I went with Louis to bury him. After the burial, the three of us rushed to the Intensive Care Unit of Maimonides Hospital to see Anna. Later, we met Barbara H. back at my parents' apartment to, "sit shiva."

I was stunned. We thought we might have to mourn both parents at once. During the days of shiva, we were at the hospital and in the evenings, we were back at the apartment where people came to offer their condolences. Several of Louis's Post Office co-workers came and told us how much they had respected his work ethic.

His integrity was his great legacy to us.

Anna steadily improved and returned to the apartment and Barbara and I went back to Connecticut. For the next few years Anna continued to blame herself, but slowly she understood that she had played no part in Louis's death. Her sadness eventually yielded to her resiliency. She would visit us in Connecticut (Ira would drive her halfway to a rest stop and we'd bring her back to New London, then reverse the process a week later). At home, she would play bingo in the neighborhood and on occasion, Izzy and she would take a day trip by bus to Atlantic City. She saw Barbara's parents frequently (Anna and Louis had moved to 140 Bay Ridge Parkway a few years before and the Robinsons lived about ten blocks away). Ira took enormously good care of her, taking her to doctors' appointments and doing her major food shopping. Grandchildren came on the scene (Lia, 1980; Jessica, 1983; Joshua, 1986) and she was delighted by them.

Anna Ages with Grace

Always in generally poor health, Anna became increasingly frail in her seventies. She had chronic back pain throughout adulthood and in later years, became legally blind like her mother. Her worries dissipated when at nearly eighty, she moved to Danbury from Brooklyn to (oddly, at her insistence) enter a nursing home. "I want to live in a place where there's a nurse outside my door," she had announced and as it turned out, she was right. She thrived there, soon becoming, "The Mayor of Hancock Hall" and eventually at her death at age 99, living there longer than any other resident.

The family at Anna's 85th birthday party, Danbury, CT, 1998

Her resiliency (she called a nursing home, "a hospital with privileges") and her outgoing nature, led her to become active in all phases of life there, even becoming the first and long-serving president of its Resident Council. Living in Danbury (where we lived at the time) gave her a wide circle of social events to attend with us, as Barbara and I were both very active in our synagogue and the school and general communities. She

149

spent quality time with her granddaughters Jessica and Lia, the latter with whom she became exceptionally close. Ira, Barbara and their young son Joshua visited frequently.

For the first time in her long life, she celebrated Christmas (the vast majority of the residents were Christian) and she couldn't get over its sights and sounds, raising record sums for the annual holiday raffle at Hancock Hall. She'd station herself in the lobby. Capitalizing on her near blindness, she'd call out to visitors who even attempted to tiptoe by her, "I can't see who you are, but I'd love to ask you to support our residents by purchasing a raffle ticket." She was a natural.

She also took up painting for the first time in her life. Working from photographs held closely to her eyes, she attended art class each week and produced many lovely works of art. At the annual resident art show and sale, she always sold a few paintings, the money going into the nursing home's resident recreation fund.

Hancock Hall put on a Senior Prom one June and I attended dressed in my tux (I could fit into it in those days) and Anna wore a

The Artist at Work

fancy dress and we danced together and drank nonalcoholic champagne. At their annual variety show, Anna was a star. She performed a variety of songs each year, but was widely known and cheered for her forceful rendition of, "Ain't She Sweet." Wearing a bow-tie and sporting a top hat, she'd strut across the stage belting out the tune. She didn't think she had much of a voice, but what she did have, was charisma.

Charisma, however, could not defeat the decline of age. At 90 she fractured her hip and required surgery. Barbara and I were in the emergency room with her and she was in a lot of pain. She wanted to know who the surgeon on call was and whether we knew him (she thought we knew everyone in Danbury). It turned out to be Dr. Elfenbein, who we did know. When he finally arrived to speak to her, she said, "Dr. Elfenbein, I've heard so many wonderful things about you." He was captivated.

She healed well from the surgery and resumed her busy schedule, but got tired of her follow-up visits to the surgeon. After several monthly visits, he told her how well she was doing and wanted to see her again in yet, another month. "Dr. Elfenbein," she said sweetly, but firmly, "I thank you for taking such good care of me, but I am doing fine now, and won't be returning" and she hobbled out of his office. Whenever I'd see him over the years we shared a laugh about Anna dismissing him.

A year later, Anna needed emergency gall bladder surgery and we were back in the emergency room. Once again, she asked who the surgeon on call was, but this time, we did not know Dr. Catania. She found that hard to believe, but quickly came up with a plan. When the surgeon finally appeared, she extended her hand and said, "Dr. Catania, I've heard so many wonderful things about you." Now, it was Dr. Catania's turn to be captivated. The surgery was successful, but instead of bringing her for a follow-up visit, Dr. Catania called me and said he knew it would be hard for her to come to his office, so he would see her at Hancock Hall. "After all," he explained, "Your mother was so nice to me in the hospital." Charisma!

Anna remained active into her mid-nineties, although by that time she was in a wheelchair. And she remained mentally sharp, charming and engaged. Most of her friendships were with staff members and they welcomed her wise and supportive advice when they were going through health or family difficulties. Her relationship with Lia deepened and when she had healed after her 90th birthday, Lia and Jessica took her out in a limo for a special lunch. She always had many visitors, some of whom were the spouses or children of residents who had died, but continued to visit Anna.

151

At age 97, plus, Anna fell, but did not require surgery. After that, she began to show signs of dementia. By the next year, she needed greater help with her daily routine, including eating, but still knew everyone in the family and on staff and was thrilled to have lived long enough to meet her great granddaughters, Haley and Briella. The aides at Hancock Hall were wonderful, but had too much to do. I was retired by then and saw her every day to help her with lunch. Lia came every evening after work

to do the same with dinner. At age 99, plus she entered the last phase of her life and her physician and my friend Dr. Charles Cahn provided loving hospice care for her at the nursing home. She did not, she had told me, want to die in a hospital. She wanted to die at Hancock Hall, she said, among friends. Death arrived shortly and peacefully, with Lia, Barbara and me in attendance. We had a graveside service at Wellwood cemetery and she is buried next to her beloved Louis.

We sat shiva at our home in Danbury and the nursing home owners, administrators, nurses and aides came to pay their respects. She had left a good name in her new community.

Not many folks live enhanced lives after entering a nursing home, but Anna did, much to her credit. She had said that if she knew she was going to live so long, she would have taken better care of herself. Instead I think, she had taken good care of everyone else. As the lyrics to her signature song said, "Yes, I ask you very confidentially, 'Ain't she sweet'."

PART TWO: MIDCENTURY MODERNS
Montauk and Erasmus

Back to the Sixties, I went to Montauk Junior High School and because I was in the SP program I skipped eighth grade, which fortunately meant I only had to go there two years, for Montauk was a pretty rough school. The SP students traveled in groups (except for physical education, art and music) as successors to the elementary IGC classes.

There were, however, some fine culinary experiences in the neighborhood after school, at least fine to teenage taste buds. To this day, over a half century later, I can still taste the heavenly Sicilian style pizza at Rose's. In the early Sixties, pizza was just starting to become popular (I don't recall pizzerias in the Fifties and we always lived in Italian/Jewish neighborhoods). I still have dreams of those rectangular doughy slices being so light that if you didn't grab one quickly, it would float up to the tin ceiling. In our own neighborhood at the tip of Dahill Road, a fast food joint (the first in the area) opened called, "The Triple Nickel." Their gimmick, as the name implies, was that everything: pizza slices, burgers, fries, hot dogs or soda was only 15 cents. It became a popular hangout for many years, but eventually when they raised their prices, the novelty wore off.

My memories of Erasmus Hall High School, a neighborhood away in Flatbush are more academic than culinary. Erasmus is the second oldest high school in the United States (Boston Latin is older), founded in 1787 as a private academy and transferred as a gift by its trustees to the City of Brooklyn (yes, Brooklyn was a separate city until 1898 when it joined NYC, a decision many Brooklynites still regret). Among the original Erasmus Hall financial supporters were colonial luminaries Alexander Hamilton, Aaron Burr, John Jay and Robert Livingston. The academy, in the heart of old Flatbush (the most important of the original 17th century Dutch villages) was named after the Dutch Renaissance humanist and Catholic theologian Desiderius Erasmus.

Statue of "Desi" in front of the 1787 Academy building, EHHS

A life-size statue (the original is in Rotterdam) resting on a pedestal guards the front of the colonial academy building. It has been a tradition for generations to throw coins up at it and if one lands on Desi's open book, one is assured of successful final exams. When I was in school, the academy building held guidance offices; small cramped offices occupied by small cramped guidance counselors.

The high school itself, resembled a medieval fortress; it's castle-like main building lording over busy, commercial Flatbush Avenue. Heavy iron gates permitted us entry as we passed through an arch into a tunnel-like opening on our way to classes. In the center of the block-long school sat a beautiful campus of lawns, flowering trees and concrete paths. It all looked like it belonged in the English countryside, rather than in dirty, noisy Flatbush. I'm telling you, that if Harry Potter had been born in Brooklyn, he'd feel right at home at Erasmus.

The Erasmus Hall High School, Flatbush Avenue Elevation

We didn't have an auditorium; we had a Chapel, and of course, it looked medieval. At the back of the stage was an enormous arched stain glass window, said to have been created by a disciple of the great Louis Comfort Tiffany; its multiple panels depicting scenes from the life of Desiderius Erasmus.

Stain glass panels at back of Chapel stage, EHHS

The chapel hosted concerts in which the young Barbra Streisand sang. When I attended the school from 1963-1966 we had already heard of her initial stage success. Streisand was one of many famous Erasmians. The school was not only old but large. At one time it was listed in "The Guiness Book of Records" as the biggest high school in the world (over 7,000 students), but had shrunk to "only" 5,200 when I was there.

Erasmus was home to many famous and accomplished alumni, including stage and screen stars Mae West, Barbara Stanwyck, Moe Howard of the Three Stooges (who dropped out after two months) and Eli Wallach, among others. I once met Eli Wallach and his actress wife Anne Jackson as we crossed

155

a busy street on the Upper West Side, coming from opposite directions. After chatting briefly mid-street, the light changed and Ms. Jackson worriedly suggested that I might want to cross quickly to safety. Besides Ms. Streisand, singer Neil Diamond, opera star Beverly Sills and record producer Clive Davis all hailed from Erasmus. From the world of sports: Olympic gold medalist and track star Cheryl Toussaint, Pro Football Hall of Famer Sid Luckman, NBA Hall of Famer Billy Cunningham and fellow member Ned Irish, founder of the New York Knicks. Writers include mystery author Mickey Spillane, sportswriter Roger Kahn and Bernard Malamud, who was awarded the Pulitzer Prize once and won the National Book Award twice.

STREISAND, BARBARA
Freshman Chorus, 1, 2; Choral Club, 2-4.

JOEL LEVITT
History Office, Dutchman Art Staff, Senior Sing, Student Assembly Representative.

"Barbara" Streisand yearbook photo, EHHS, 1959:
Joel Levitt EHHS yearbook photo, 1966

When I taught there, from 1971-1976, the teacher in charge of the literary magazine, "The Erasmian" received a letter and a generous check from Malamud (then already well known) to ensure that any work he had written as a student would never be released to the public.

At Erasmus I became seriously interested in art and had some wonderful, influential teachers. Fred Levenson was the always harried, but well- respected chair of the Art Dept. Erica Glidden, my painting teacher, was lots of fun, very caring and a very discombobulated teacher. As a kid, I used to organize her paperwork; taking attendance, ordering supplies, etc. She was an influence in my becoming an art teacher. When I did return as an art teacher after a short stint teaching at Pershing Junior High School (Anna's alma mater), we became good friends. She had much disappointment and even tragedy in her life, but she never lost her anti-establishment spirit, nor sense of hope.

Ed Henrion, my old drawing teacher and mentor, and his wife Marilyn, a noted quilt artist also became friends. Jim Meade, a watercolorist, was my cooperating teacher when I was a student teacher and he was a soft-spoken, patient man and excellent advisor. Fred the department. chair, harried when I was a student, was even more harried when I returned as a teacher, but he was a decent, hard-working man.

The principal during the last few years of my brief tenure, Harriet Oxman called me into her office one day (being summoned to see Mrs. Oxman could provoke fear in any one: student or faculty). She told me that I would replace Fred as department head after his retirement (he had not announced a date yet, nor even a year) and I was to apply to the administration program at Brooklyn College to get certified. I nervously thanked her, but said that I had only recently entered teaching (I must have been 25 at the time), loved it and really didn't want to be an administrator (I have a feeling that my voice might have cracked when I said that). She dismissed me and said to think about it.

I went home to Barbara and explained what had happened. Barbara, having heard of Mrs. Oxman's reputation, said that if she wanted me to become an administrator, I had better apply to Brooklyn College, and so I did. The truth is that Mrs. Oxman saw something in me that I myself, did not. I became an arts administrator at age 30, but not at Erasmus, and continued in that profession until I retired 30 years later. I had loved being a teacher, but saw great value and impact in being an administrator; a career I truly loved, as well.

Mrs. Oxman, by the way, attained her toughness because she had to. She was one of the few women serving as high school principals in NYC at the time. She had risen through the ranks as teacher, grade advisor and assistant principal and it surely had been difficult for her along the way.

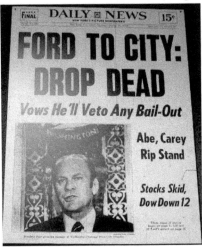

About midway into my administration coursework at Brooklyn College, I received a layoff notice from the NYC Board of Education. It was not a surprise, as successive years of fiscal troubles had put the City in danger of bankruptcy and each year of my career had seen teacher layoffs. The situation was dire and Pres. Ford refused to provide federal financial aid to NYC.

Infamous "Daily News" headline during NYC fiscal crisis

Even though I was tenured, every art teacher in the City with under eight years was laid off over a period of a few years. Mrs. Oxman was kind enough to hold an English teaching vacancy for me and I immediately recertified in that field, but that too, was cut from the school.

I was devastated, but Barbara and I determined that this might provide an opportunity to live elsewhere, as all we had known was Brooklyn. NYC was so different and difficult in the Seventies than it is today. The City was in a constant state of economic distress, crime was rampant, drug use high, garbage everywhere, subways crowded and dirty. Municipal workers were often on strike (I had been involved in a teachers' union strike the year before, walked the picket lines and had been fined two days' pay for every day on strike, under the Taylor Law, but I was proud to walk the line for teacher rights). We made the decision to leave Brooklyn for Connecticut.

Barbara & Joel Meet at Hillel

In between being a student (1962-1966) at Erasmus and a teacher at Erasmus (1971-1976) I was a student at Brooklyn College, or in many ways, a student at the Hillel Foundation at Brooklyn College, at the time, the world's largest Hillel. I had never been involved in a Jewish organization before: never went to Jewish summer camp, spent almost no time in synagogue after Hebrew School and Bar Mitzvah, never joined a Jewish youth group. Hillel changed that. I went to a freshman reception, liked the people and became involved. By my sophomore year, I chaired the Publicity Committee and like all committee chairs, was encouraged to meet incoming freshmen at their reception. I also figured it might be a good place to meet girls.

Barbara and Joel: The Early Years

On Sept. 17, 1967, across the reception hall, I spotted a beautiful red-haired freshman talking to a fellow sophomore; a man short of stature, but not of ego, who while still a teenager tried to affect the look of an English prof by smoking a pipe and wearing a corduroy jacket with elbow patches. You can tell

I didn't care for him. I walked over to her, introduced myself and rescued her from the twit.

Barbara and I immediately hit it off, although she was quite shy. For those of you who know her and don't believe that, I repeat: Barbara was quite shy. We (more likely I) spoke at length and I asked if she would like to join my publicity committee. She gave me her address. She was 16 and I was 18. We have been a couple ever since (over 51 years and God-willing, many, many more).

I sent her a postcard to invite her to our first meeting, but although I got the address right, I screwed up her last name, mailing it to Barbara Robertson, instead of Barbara Robinson. Although she lived in a large apartment house, her mail carrier knew that fellow mail carrier, resident Harry Robinson had a daughter named Barbara and so delivered it to her mailbox (my father also worked in the Post Office, so I guess the PO Angels were looking down on us). She saved the postcard.

Original postal card with incorrect last name for Barbara, Sept. 21, 1967

Meeting each other and our years together at Hillel turned out to be a defining experience for us.

The adult leadership at Hillel believed in giving students increased responsibilities as we gained more experience. Because it was such a large organization, we sponsored a multitude of events; from lectures with well-known authors to concerts and theatrical productions, Jewish holiday programs, overnight seminars, religious services, marches to promote the free emigration of Soviet Jewry and support for Israel, etc. Barbara and I jumped right in. Moreover, the amazing directors, Rabbi Dr. Norman Frimer and Rabbi Frank Fischer had the ability to sit back and let us make our own mistakes, yet also help us learn from them. We learned to mature.

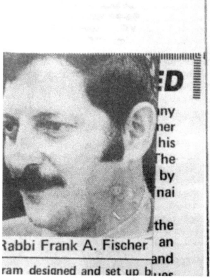 

Rabbis Fischer and Frimer

Hillel friends for life, from left: Morris and Debbie Finkelstein, Joel and Barbara Levitt, Judy and Michael Turk, ca. 1970s

Through Hillel, we discovered that Judaism could become central to our lives and that gave us a powerful foundation for social activism among all races, ethnicities and faiths in every community we've lived in. Most of all, though, Barbara and I fell in love there.

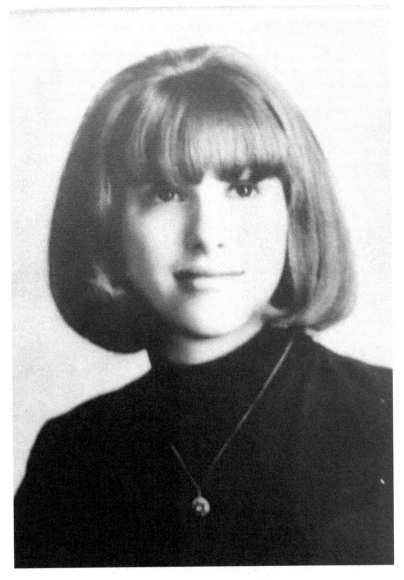

Barbara Robinson, ca. 1967

The Robinsons:
My Second Family Through Marriage

Kay and Harry Robinson

It wasn't long after I met Barbara, that I was introduced to her parents, Kay and Harry Robinson (not Robertson!), a stay-at-home Mom and a postal worker, just like my parents. Kay was a warm, friendly woman of simple tastes. She was an obsessive house cleaner, even leaning out the windows (they lived on the third floor) to wash the city grime off the panes of glass. On Fridays, floor-washing day, you had to hop from newspaper to newspaper placed on the newly washed and waxed linoleum to get from one room to the next.

Harry, Kay and Barbara Robinson, ca. 1950s

Harry was a democratic socialist (like my Uncle Isadore) and a lover of history, mathematics, folk music, and politics. He was intensely against the Vietnam War, which made him popular among our friends. As a young man, he had run unsuccessfully for a seat in the NYS Assembly. His stereo system (which he prized) was constantly cranking out the likes of Phil Ochs, Peter, Paul and Mary, Tom Paxton, Woody Guthrie, Pete Seeger and other folk greats. A kind and considerate gentleman, he never said a bad word against anyone, except presidents Lyndon B. Johnson and Richard Nixon, who he blamed for the war. He was also the most nervous human being I have ever met.

As Barbara and I become closer, so did Kay and Harry and Anna and Louis. After we married, I'd say they developed into each couple's closest friends. To this day, I have never seen "machetunim" (in-laws) as genuinely close and caring for

Kay and Harry Robinson, 1972

each other in any other marriage. While that was a remarkable and wonderful development, the combination of Anna's anxiety coupled with Harry's nervousness could be stultifying. Moving to Connecticut gave us a break, but not entirely.

We visited Brooklyn frequently, especially after Louis died. When we'd head back home, Harry would insist that we call him as soon as we set our luggage down in Connecticut, to assure him of our safe return. We should do that, he would explain, only because Anna would be worried. Anna in turn, would tell us to do the same, because we knew how nervous Harry was. It was a conspiracy!

In those days, long-distance calls were expensive and even though each offered to pay for it, we chafed under what we considered smothering control. We reached a compromise. We would call the Robinsons once we arrived home, making a person-to-person call asking for Barbara Robinson. Harry would answer, telling the operator that she was not home, so we wouldn't get charged for the call. Knowing that we had arrived home safely (at least safe enough to hear Barbara's voice), he'd immediately call Anna to reassure her that all was well.

When Anna and Louis lived on Dahill Road, Harry, whose post office was only a few short blocks away, would sometimes stop by for lunch. Louis, in turn, would drive them places on weekends. After the move to Bay Ridge and widowhood for both (they lived about 10 blocks from each other), Kay would sometimes do Anna's shopping as it became more difficult for her to get out. They called each other every day. The Levitts and Robinsons were perfect complements for each other: decent, honest, hardworking and loving people.

An only child born later in their lives, Barbara was their world. It was that simple. My relationship with my in-laws also turned out to be very simple. They loved me and I loved them. We were all very fortunate.

Brooklyn College

We became so deeply involved in Hillel, that at times Brooklyn College itself almost seemed like an afterthought. Still, I became an art major and Barbara, an education major. We both joined house plans (a poorer version of sororities and fraternities); Barbara at Joy House and me, at Maxwell House and worked on Country Fair, an annual festival of floats and fun activities. Like so many generations of students, we crowded into The Sugar Bowl, the local luncheonette

Brooklyn College Country Fair: Louis, Anna, Barbara, Joel, Ira, 1968

Louis had told me apologetically, that he couldn't afford to send me to a private college, so Brooklyn College, it was. As part of the City University of New York, there was no charge for tuition. Along with City College in Manhattan, it was a prestigious institution with high standards for entry. I was awarded a NYS Regents Scholarship for the maximum annual amount; $350 a year, which covered all of my textbooks and art supplies. Ira joined us at Brooklyn College after two years at Kingsborough Community College, where decades later, he became an adjunct professor.

Barbara, Ira and I all worked during college. Ira was at the Raleigh Hotel in the Catskills every weekend and summer. Barbara worked summers as an assistant to the advertising director at her local weekly newspaper, "The (Bay Ridge) Home Reporter." Through Hillel connections, I had well-paying summer jobs, first as a janitor at a factory in the Garment Center in Manhattan and then for the next three summers as a freight elevator operator in a factory in the Fur Market at 130 W. 30 St.

Cleaning bathrooms from the 18th floor to the lobby was a great lesson for me. I had never had a job in high school and never thought I'd be wearing a dirt-gray uniform each day and doing filthy hard work, overseen by a head custodian who was not happy to be saddled with a college student. I guess my motivation was to prove him wrong. I took pride in keeping 18 stories of factory workers' bathrooms clean and polished the brass fittings in the front lobby to a brilliant sheen, where the executives and models used to enter.

The Fur Market job I really enjoyed. My fellow freight elevator operators were working-class guys from Puerto Rico and they were welcoming, lively and loudly profane. Since the fur pelts were delivered through the freight entrance, I soon learned to tell the difference between mink, chinchilla, fox, etc. (I was not a vegetarian then).

My college working days taught me the value of working hard, no matter what the job. It was my first actual working experience and I'm grateful it had a formative impact on me. And once I caught the working bug I just continued working.

No backpacking across Europe, etc., just working to save money for our future apartment rent and furnishings. In total, I was employed for about 40 years until retirement and enjoyed it all!

At one point, I saw union goons push around a fur deliverer, who I guess had angered local officials. Soon after, they came to me and said I had to join and pay dues to local 32B of the service employees union. They threatened to pull me off the job, if I didn't. I did, under an arrangement where I paid dues only for the months I worked and was actually pretty proud to be a part of a union. I was an active union member for my entire teaching and administrative career, as well.

The Graduates, 1970

Ira, on the other hand, was a hard worker from age 16. His initial grocery job found him doing strenuous work in the basement of the supermarket. In those days, you didn't want to see a supermarket basement (probably not today, either). Later, he worked above ground in the appetizing and cheese department. When he worked to the Raleigh Hotel, he assumed more and more responsibility, assisting his school principal, who was also in charge of the summer and weekend workers at the hotel, and who grew to lean on him for help.

We both had grown up under the same circumstances concerning money, but had different responses. That money was tight was a "leitmotif" of our childhood. Whether we realized it or not, four people living in three rooms, Ira and I sleeping on foam slabs and all of us, sharing a bathroom with strangers reinforced the feeling that we were not yet living "The American Dream." My parents' agreement was that Louis would turn over his check to Anna and that she would give him an "allowance" while she would manage the family's finances. While we knew we were not poor, we understood that we were definitely on the lower end of "lower middle-class."

The political climate in the United States at the time was at a boil as the Vietnam War took center stage. There were student protests against the war on campuses throughout the country, but at BC, a commuter school with a largely lower middle-class student population of first and second-generation strivers, the protests were more muted. Draft deferments were offered nationally for men who became teachers and so Ira became an elementary education major like Barbara and I became an art major/ed minor, which would qualify me to teach art.

Ira student taught at PS 94 in the Sunset Park neighborhood of Brooklyn, where he spent his entire 35-year career and was enormously popular with generations of students and parents. I student taught at Erasmus. I had a great time student teaching and was given full responsibility for my classes.

My first regular teaching position in September, 1970, was at Pershing Junior High School, where I spent one unhappy semester. Pershing seemed to be run more like a school for wayward children in Dickensian London than 1970 Brooklyn. It was a tough school and it was a tough age for kids, but there appeared to be little empathy from the school administration and no mentoring of new teachers like myself. One day the principal called me out of class and into the hall (while I was teaching!) to sternly inform me not to smile at the students (he had peeped through the window in the door and caught me in the act). When we returned from December vacation, my former cooperating teacher Jim Meade called to tell me that an art teacher was retiring at

Erasmus midyear and that they wanted me to replace her. I jumped at the opportunity.

In the near decade since I had entered Erasmus as a freshman, it had undergone a rapid change. No longer a bastion of "movers and shakers" of the middle class, it had become a much poorer and less integrated school, reflecting the changing demographics of many older Brooklyn neighborhoods. It was an era of fights over control of the schools through a process called, "decentralization," school system strikes and parent boycotts, racial antagonism (while the public schools now had a majority of minority students, the teachers and principals were overwhelmingly white and the majority, Jewish). It was the period of Black Power and African nationalism (many of my students incorporated the liberation colors of red, black and green into their artwork). I loved teaching there and had many excellent relationships with my students, a couple of whom I'm still in touch with (during a particularly turbulent time an African-American girl in one of my classes, reassured me by confiding, "Don't worry Mr. Levitt. When the Revolution comes, you'll be spared"). I don't think I've received a more genuine compliment, since.

Barbara student taught at a school in Sunset Park, the same one that Ira taught at, but took a job back at BC as an administrative assistant to Dr. Bela Kiraly, the History Department chair.

Bela was one of the most remarkable people we have known and became a close friend. He had been a field general during the Hungarian Revolution and a war hero imprisoned and marked for death by the Communists. During World War ll, his intercession saved the lives of many Hungarian Jews and *The General in uniform* his name and deeds are enshrined at Yad Vashem, the national Israeli Holocaust Museum as a "Righteous Gentile Among the Nations": its highest honor to those who had saved Jewish lives. Yet he was incredibly modest and enormously charming (he

171

kissed the hand of every woman he met). We used to visit him at his book-lined weekend place in northern New Jersey, where he raised pigeons: this great man who had saved lives and undoubtedly taken lives during wartime, relaxed by stroking and whispering to his cooing collection of birds, just as he had done as a child in his beloved Hungary. He was one of a kind.

While at Brooklyn College, Barbara and I had our first date shortly after meeting. I went to her apartment with flowers in hand (my first date strategy was always to bring flowers).

I had tickets to the world-famous Moscow Circus at Madison Square Garden in Manhattan. We shared a chaste kiss (perhaps, not so chaste) at the door to her apartment afterwards and our relationship was off and running.

Barbara's gravity-defying hairstyle. I began to dress like an English prof, myself

We dated steadily for several years, falling in love and becoming engaged. My parents took me to their longtime friend, jeweler Morris Papier (his wife Mae, a "Lerner girl" had been Anna's maid of honor), a very nice man I had known all my life. He suggested that a smaller diamond without visible flaws was better than a larger, flashier, yet flawed stone and I took his advice. I proposed to Barbara in our car parked near her office. We immediately went to show her parents the ring, then the four of us went to my parents' apartment. When she returned home, she started making calls to her girlfriends.

Tada!

Our engagement party was held in the basement recreation room of the building where Victoria Confino (remember her?) lived with her daughter Celia and her son-in-law Stanley. "What goes around, comes around."

Engaged

Barbara and I got married at the Laurelton Jewish Center in Queens on April 8, 1973.

Barbara and Joel. April 8, 1973

*Left: Lia Levitt, 2017. Right: Jessica and Joseph
Bittner, 2006*

Our lives together these past 45 years of marriage, and those of our beautiful and accomplished daughters Lia Jill (b. March 8, 1980) and Jessica Taryn (b. May 26, 1983) and her wonderful husband Joseph Bittner and our darling grandchildren, twins Haley Shianne and Briella Kylee (b. June 12, 2011) and Joseph Ashton, called Joey (b. Dec. 15, 2016); well, that's a story for another time (perhaps Volume Two). But it is for Haley, Briella and Joey and their descendants, that I've spun this golden tale.

Over a century later, Joel and Barbara, Briella and Haley retraced our families' arrival in America at the Statue of Liberty and Ellis Island, 2018

And so, this story of the Past, told in the Present, concludes with the Future.

Joel and Barbara, Briella and Haley at the Statue of Liberty, 2018

Briella, Joey and Haley Bittner, 2017

Family Trees

The Levitt Family

1 **Leib Levitt**, (ca. 1855-ca.1910), b. Ostrovets or Velizh, Belarus, m. (name unknown), res. Ostrovets, Belarus, Vitebsk, Belarus

  2 **Jacob Levitt**, (ca.1880-1950), m. ca. 1903 Sarah Czenzov (ca. 1884-1958), b. Ostrovets or Velizh, Belarus, res. Vitebsk, Belarus, Brooklyn, NY

    3 **Elinor (Anna) Levitt**, (1905-1987), b. Vitebsk, Belarus, m. 1928 Isadore Axelrod, (1895-1988) res. Vitebsk, Belarus, Baltimore, MD, Atlantic City, NJ, Brooklyn, NY

    3 **Alex Levitt**, (1907-1963), m. Lillian Lustman (1902-1999) b. Vitebsk, Belarus, res. Queens, NY, Los Angeles, CA (Lillian)

      4 **Paul D. Levitt**, (1940-) m. 1962 Leslie Bellet (1941-) res. Beverly Hills, CA, Newport Coast, CA

        5 **Amy Levitt**, (1963-) m. Pablo Polanco, res. Los Angeles, CA

          6 **Jessie Levitt-Polanco**, (2008-)

          6 **Eli Levitt-Polanco**, (2010-)

        5 **Deborah Levitt**, (1967-) m. Edward Malters, res. Billings, MT

          6 **Joshua Malters**, (1996-)

          6 **Zoe Malters**, (1998-)

        5 **Marc Levitt**, (1973-) m. Petra Czank, res. Las Vegas, NV

          6 **Benjamin Levitt**, (2015-)

          6 **Alex Levitt**, (2016-)

          6 **Lillian Levitt**, (2016-)

      4 **Renie Levitt**, (1946-), m. Arthur Bailyn, div. res. Carlsbad, CA

        5 **Eric Bailyn**, (1967-) m. 1996 Laurie Ehrlich (1968-) res. Carlsbad, CA

          6 **David Bailyn**, (1998-)

          6 **Noah Bailyn**, (1999-)

        5 **Jill Bailyn**, (1968-) res. Laguna Woods, CA

    3 **Louis Levitt**, (1911-1978) Brooklyn, NY, m. Anne, (?-?), div. res. Brooklyn, NY

    *2nd wife of **Louis Levitt** m.1947 Anna Kaplan, (1913-2012), res. Brooklyn, NY, Danbury CT (Anna)

4 **Ira Stephen Levitt,** (1948-) m. 1977 Barbara Ann Harfosh, (1951-) res. Brooklyn, NY

   5 **Joshua Michael Levitt,** (1986-) m. Melissa Wu (1988-), res. Brooklyn, NY

4 **Joel Stanley Levitt (Yoel ben Leib),** (1949-) m. 1973 Barbara Lee Robinson (Bracha Tzivia), res. Brooklyn, NY, New London, CT, Niantic, CT, Danbury, CT, New Milford, CT

   5 **Lia Jill Levitt (Liba Yochebed),** (1980-) res. Danbury, CT, Sandy Hook, CT

   5 **Jessica Taryn Levitt (Chaya Tova),** (1983-) m. 2006 Joseph Henry Bittner, b. 1983, res. Danbury, CT, New Milford, CT

      6 **Haley Shianne Bittner (Hila Serafina),** (2011-) res. New Milford, CT

      6 **Briella Kylee Bittner (Brielle Kayla),** (2011-), res. New Milford, CT

      6 **Joseph (Joey) Ashton Bittner (Yosef Asher),** (2016-), res. New Milford, CT

3 **Shirley Levitt,** (1913-1981), Brooklyn, NY, m. 1939 Sheppard Davis, (1907-1989) res. Brooklyn, NY, Paterson, NJ, Miami, FL

   4 **Jacqueline Davis,** (1952-) m. 1970 Joel Rosenthal (1950-1996), res. Paterson, NJ Miami, FL

      5 **Edward B. Rosenthal** (1971-) w. Lynn Carter, res. Davie, FL

      5 **Scott L. Rosenthal** (1974-) m. 2018 Marla West, res. Sorrento, FL

     ⋆2nd husband of **Jacqueline Davis Rosenthal** m. 2008 Daniel Schwartz (1955-), res. Sorrento, FL

   4 **Charles K. Davis,** (1955-?) res. Paterson, NJ, Hollywood, FL

3 **Hyman Levitt** (1914-1994) Brooklyn, NY, m. Annamollie Davis, (1921-?) div. res. Queens, NY

   4 **Michael D. Levitt,** (1939-1997) m. Suzanne Grossman (1945-1982), div. res. Queens, NY

      5 **Scott E. Levitt,** (1964-), m. 1997 Wilma Stinson (1945-) res. Ocoee, FL

      5 **Gary Alan Levitt,** (1968-), m. 2000 Elena Campiri, div. res. Lindenhurst, NY

         6 **Jacob Levitt** (2002-)

     ⋆2nd wife of **Michael D. Levitt** m. Arlene (?-?)

4 **Charles Levitt,** (1942-) m. Joyce Norstein, (1943-1991) div., res. Queens, NY

    5 **Joelle Levitt** (1966-) m. Michael Mangiafico, div.

        6 **Sofia Joy Mangiafico,** (2002-), res. Pittsburgh, PA

        ★2nd husband of **Joelle Levitt** m. Scott Killebrew, res. Pittsburgh, PA

        6 **Sydney Anna Killebrew** (2004-), res. Pittsburgh, PA

    5 **Nicole (Nikki) Levitt** (1969-) m. Michael Schrift (1966-), div. res. Beaverton, OR

        6 **Jacob Schrift,** (1998-), res. Beaverton, OR

        6 **Kyle Schrift,** (2001-) res. Beaverton, OR

★2nd wife of **Charles Levitt** m. Milagra Ortega-Rodriguez, (1947-2013) res. Glenview, IL

    5 **Matthew Abraham Levitt,** (1974-) res. Mt. Prospect, IL

    5 **Joshua Adam Levitt,** (1979-) m. Georgia Hetherington (1980-), div. res. Roselle, IL

        6 **Jaylen Levitt** (2001-), res. Roselle, IL

        6 **Jacob Adam Levitt** (2005-), res. Roselle, IL

★2nd wife of **Hyman Levitt** m. 1972 Anne Sterman (1950-), res. Queens, NY

    4 **David Levitt,** (1970-) m. Claudia Reyes, div. res. Queens, NY

    5 **Lauren Levitt,** (1995-), res. Queens, NY

★2nd husband of Anne Sterman Levitt m. 1996 Gary Kroll (1949-), res. Amityville, NY

Tillie Musicant (Muzykant) Kaplan Family Tree

1 **Rafael (Folik) HaLevy Muzykant,** (?-bef. 1860) m. ?
res. Tarashcha, Ukraine

  2 **Leib Baer Muzykant** (ca. 1840- bef. 1906) m. Hanah, res. Tarashcha,
Ukraine

    3 **Taube (Tillie) Musicant** (ca. 1876-1956) m. Yehudah Lib
HaKohane (?-bef.1906), res. Tarashcha, Ukraine, The Bronx,
NY, Brooklyn, NY

      4 **Morris Musicant (Kaplan)** (1895-1967) adopted ca. 1910
by Isaac Kaplan m. Gertrude Rosenthal (ca. 1894-1967)
res. Tarashcha, Ukraine, The Bronx, NY, Brooklyn, NY

        5 **Lillian Kaplan** (1918-2008) m. 1938 Samuel Goodman
(1911-2001) res. Brooklyn, NY

          6 **Paulette Goodman** (1940-) m. 1959 Saul Weinstein
(1938-?) div. res. Brooklyn, NY, Parsippany, NJ

            7 **Tori Sue Weinstein** (1961-) res. Brooklyn, NY,
Chatham, NJ

            7 **Cindy Ellen Weinstein** (1963-) m. 1988 Jeffrey
Blustein (1957-), div. res. Brooklyn, NY,
Livingston, NJ, Florham Park, NJ

              8 **Emily Rose Blustein** (1992-) m. 2018
Gabriel Pesso (1989-) res. New York, NY

              8 **Andrew Jeremy Blustein** (1995-) res.
New Brunswick, NJ

            *2nd husband of **Paulette Goodman** m. 1973 Jack
Edelson (1938-2004), res. Mountain Lakes, NJ

          6 **Michael Goodman** (1944-?) m. Rita Zeiger (1947-)
res. Brooklyn, NY

            7 **Lisa Ellen Goodman** (1980-) res. Las Vegas, NV

        5 **Joseph Kaplan** (1920-1984) m. 1955 Ethel Moldauer,
div. res. Brooklyn, NY

          6 **Terry B. Kaplan** (1956-) m. Martha Farfan (1955-)
res. New York, NY

          *2nd wife of **Terry Kaplan** m. Constanza Melo
(1961-) res. Brooklyn, NY

          6 **Harvey B. Kaplan** (1959-) m. Janet? div. res.
Brooklyn, NY

          *2nd wife of **Harvey Kaplan** m. Sunisa Thavisin
res. Brooklyn, NY

    *2nd husband of **Tillie Musicant** m. 1908 Isaac Kaplan b. Grodno,
Belarus (ca. 1860-1931), res. The Bronx, NY, Brooklyn, NY

4 **Anna Kaplan** (1913-2012) m. 1946 Louis Levitt (1911-1978), res. Brooklyn

    5 **Ira Stephen Levitt,** (1948-) m. 1977 Barbara Ann Harfosh, (1951-) res. Brooklyn, NY

        6 **Joshua Michael Levitt,** (1986-) m.2018 Melissa Wu (1988-), res. Brooklyn, NY

    5 **Joel Stanley Levitt,** (1949-) m. 1973 Barbara Lee Robinson, (1950-) res. Brooklyn, NY, New London, CT, Danbury, CT, New Milford, CT

        6 **Lia Jill Levitt,** (1980-) res. New London, CT, Danbury, CT, Sandy Hook, CT

        6 **Jessica Taryn Levitt,** (1983-) m. 2006 Joseph Henry Bittner, (1983), res. Danbury, CT, New Milford, CT

            7 **Haley Shianne Bittner,** (2011-) res. New Milford, CT

            7 **Briella Kylee Bittner,** (2011-), res. New Milford, CT

            7 **Joseph (Joey) Ashton Bittner,** (2016-), res. New Milford, CT

Kaplan/Bromberg Family Tree

1 **Himan Kaplan** b.(ca.1840s) Grodno, Belarus m. Eavie Appelbaum (b.ca. 1940s),res. Grodno, Belarus

  2 **Isaac Kaplan,** b. Grodno, Belarus (ca.1861-1931), m.? res. Grodno/ Chomsk, Belarus m. 1908 Tillie Musicant, b. Tarashcha, Belarus d. res. Brooklyn, NY

    3 **Fannie Kaplan** b. Chomsk, Belarus (ca.1881-1974) m. 1903 Carl Bromberg, b. Kiev, Ukraine (1876-1949), res. Brooklyn, NY

      4 **Ethel Bromberg,** (1909-1997) m. 1933 Louis Golden, (1907-) res. Brooklyn, NY, Delray Beach, FL

        5 **Eileen Golden,** (1934-) m. Murray Hetson, (1930-2013) res. Roslyn, NY, Lake Worth, FL

          6 **Joanne Hetson,** (1956-) m. Eric Harrison, res. Grand Rapids, MI

            7 **Dana Harrison,** (1986-) res. Ft. Worth, TX

            7 **David Harrison,** (1986-) res. Grand Rapids, MI

          6 **Wendy Hetson,** (1960-) m. Joseph Ehrlich, res. Jericho, NY, Highland Beach, FL

            7 **Benjamin Ehrlich** (1991-). res. New York, NY

            7 **Sarah Ehrlich,** (1993-) res. New York, NY

        5 **Samuel Golden,** (1940-), m. Terri Schwarz (1947-), res. Boynton Beach, FL

          6 **Mark Golden,** (1970-) (m. Melissa, res. Wellington, FL

            7 **Scott Golden,** (

            7 **Brett Golden,** (

          6 **Kevin Golden,** (1973-), m. Caryn Lefkowitz, res. Montvale, NJ

            7 **Lia Golden,** (

            7 **Marli Golden,** (

      4 **Oscar Bromberg** (1912-1996) m. Pearl Lisinsky (1923-2018), res. Queens, NY

        5 **Kenneth Bromberg** (1949-) m. Maryann Hodge, res. Brooklyn, NY

          6 **Johanna Bromberg** (1977-) m. Wesley Craig, res. Charlottesville, VA

            7 **Zara Craig** (2005-)

            7 **Amity Craig** (2010-)

*Kenneth Bromberg m. Philippa Gordon (1954-), res. Brooklyn, NY

   6 **Sophie Bromberg** (1990-)

   6 **Annie Bromberg** (1993-)

   6 **Eve Bromberg** (1996-)

5 **Deborah Bromberg** (1952-) m. 1998 James Stanfield (1961-), res. Rutherfordton, NC

   6 —

*2nd wife of Isaac Kaplan m. 1908 Tillie Musicant b. Tarashcha, Ukraine (ca. 1876-1956), res. The Bronx, NY, Brooklyn, NY

   3 **Anna Kaplan** (1913-2012) m. 1946 Louis Levitt (1911-1978), res. Brooklyn

      4 **Ira Stephen Levitt**, (1948-) m. 1977 Barbara Ann Harfosh, (1951-) res. Brooklyn, NY

         5 **Joshua Michael Levitt**, (1986) -m. Melissa Wu (), res. Brooklyn, NY

      4 **Joel Stanley Levitt**, (1949-) m. 1973 Barbara Lee Robinson, (1950-) res. Brooklyn, NY, New London, CT, Danbury, CT, New Milford, CT

         5 **Lia Jill Levitt**, (1980-) res. New London, CT, Danbury, CT, Sandy Hook, CT

         5 **Jessica Taryn Levitt**, (1983-) m. 2006 Joseph Henry Bittner, (1983), res. Danbury, CT, New Milford, CT

            6 **Haley Shianne Bittner**, (2011-) res. New Milford, CT

            6 **Briella Kylee Bittner**, (2011-), res. New Milford, CT

            6 **Joseph (Joey) Ashton Bittner**, (2016-), res. New Milford, CT

Kaplan (Hartford) Family Tree

1 **Himan Kaplan** b. ca. 1830s Grodno, Belarus, m. Eavie Appelbaum b. ca. 1830s, res. Grodno, Belarus

  2 **Isaac Kaplan** b. Grodno, Belarus (ca. 1861-1931) m. Dora, res. Grodno, Belarus, Chomsk, Belarus

    3 **Benjamin Morris Kaplan** (1889-1969) Chomsk, Belarus. Rebecca Kamins (1888-1978), res. Hartford, CT, West Hartford, CT, Bloomfield, CT

      4 **Alexander David Kaplan** (1916-1966) m. 1945 Nettie Frank (1921-2012), res. Bloomfield, CT

        5 **Richard Frank Kaplan** (1948-) m. 2003 Sherry Steinmetz(1960-) res. Woodbridge, CT

          6 **Jenn Markel Smith** (1967-) m.? res. Westminster, CO

            7 **Emily Smith** (1997-)

            7 **Henry Smith** (2000-)

        5 **David Gershwin Kaplan** (1951-) res. West Hartford, CT

          6 **Daniel Kaplan** (1987-) res. Hartford, CT

            7 **Kerry Kaplan** (2015-) res. Dominican Republic

        5 **Deborah Laurie Kaplan** (1955-) m. 1991 Luis Brindis (1957-), res. Lanesville, NY

          6 **Alexander Emiliano Brindis** (1992-), res. New York, NY

          6 **Diego Andres Brindis** (1995-) res. New York, NY

      4 **Henry Morris Kaplan** (1919-) m. Rhoda Baskin, res. New Britain, CT, Clinton, CT

        5 **Ronald Kaplan** (1953-) m. Randi Musnitsky, res. Warren, NJ

        5 **Norman Kaplan** (1953-) m. Laura, res. Milford, CT

          6 **Jonathan Hollander Kaplan**

        5 **Robert Kalman Kaplan** (1956-) m. Judith Bernstein, res. Clinton, CT

          6 **Benjamin Kaplan** (1987-) res. Clinton, CT

        ★2nd wife of **Robert Kaplan** m. Lisa Brownell Walker (1968-), res. Clinton, CT

          6 **Olivia Kaplan** (2003-), res. Clinton, CT

          6 **Samuel Kaplan** (2005-) res. Clinton, CT

        5 **Michael Jay Kaplan** (1960-) m. 1993, Stacy Chorches (1964-), res. Woodbridge, CT

      6 **Eliana Rebecca Kaplan** (1997-)

      6 **Maxwell Josiah Kaplan** (1997-)

      6 **Zachary Abraham Kaplan** (1997-)

      6 **Alexa Gabriel Kaplan** (1999-)

      6 **Isabella Chaya Kaplan** (2003-)

*2nd wife of **Isaac Kaplan** m. 1908 Tillie Musicant b. Tarashcha, Ukraine (ca. 1876-1956), res. The Bronx, NY, Brooklyn, NY

  3 **Anna Kaplan** (1913-2012) m. 1946 Louis Levitt (1911-1978), res. Brooklyn

    4 **Ira Stephen Levitt**, (1948-) m. 1977 Barbara Ann Harfosh, (1951-) res. Brooklyn, NY

      5 **Joshua Michael Levitt**, (1986) -m. Melissa Wu (), res. Brooklyn, NY

    4 **Joel Stanley Levitt**, (1949-) m. 1973 Barbara Lee Robinson, (1950-) res. Brooklyn, NY, New London, CT, Danbury, CT, New Milford, CT

      5 **Lia Jill Levitt**, (1980-) res. New London, CT, Danbury, CT, Sandy Hook, CT

      5 **Jessica Taryn Levitt**, (1983-) m. 2006 Joseph Henry Bittner, (1983), res. Danbury, CT, New Milford, CT

        6 **Haley Shianne Bittner**, (2011-) res. New Milford, CT

        6 **Briella Kylee Bittner**, (2011-), res. New Milford, CT

        6 **Joseph (Joey) Ashton Bittner**, (2016-), res. New Milford, CT

The Kaplan Brothers Family Tree

JULIUS KAPLAN

1 **Himan Kaplan** b. ca. 1830s Grodno, Belarus, m. Eavie Appelbaum, b. ca. 1830s res. Grodno, Belarus

  2 **Isaac Kaplan** b. Grodno, Belarus (ca. 1861-1931) m.?, res. Grodno/ Chomsk, Belarus, Brooklyn, NY

    3 **Julius Kaplan** (ca. 1886-1976), Chomsk, Belarus, m. Rae ? (1900-1980), res. Brooklyn, NY

      4 **Jack (Jerry) Kaplan** (1920-?), m. Bernice, res. Long Island, NY

        5 **Alan Kaplan** (ca. 1945-), res. Oceanside, NY, Orlando, FL

        5 **Ronald Kaplan** (ca. 1945-) res. Oceanside, NY

        5 **Andrew Kaplan** ? res. Oceanside, NY

      4 **Edward Kaplan** (ca. 1925-?) m. Kay ? res. Winsted, CT

JOSEPH KAPLAN

1 **Himan Kaplan** b. ca. 1830s Grodno, Belarus, m. Eavie Appelbaum, b. ca. 1830s res. Grodno, Belarus

  2 **Isaac Kaplan** b. Grodno, Belarus (ca. 1861-1931) m.?, res. Grodno, Belarus, Chomsk, Belarus, Brooklyn, NY

    3 **Joseph Kaplan** (ca. 1885-1942) m. Celia Gordon (ca. 1883-1970), res. Chomsk, Belarus, Brooklyn, NY, Amityville, NY

      4 **Nathaniel (Nat) Kaplan** (1911-1979) m.(1970s) Eleanor? res. Poughkeepsie, Spring Valley, New York, NY, d. Naples FL

      4 **Arthur (Archie) Kaplan** (1915-1998) m. 1945 Phyllis Richtman (1923- 2011), Amityville, NY, New Milford, NJ, Delray Beach, FL

        5 **Joanne Susan Kaplan** (1948-) m. 1986 James Handloser, (1942-) res. New Milford, NJ, New York, NY, Sagaponack, NY

      4 **Philip Kaplan** (1919? 1925?-2011) m. Lynn (1931-2011) div. res. NJ. Ft. Myers, FL

        5 **Jan Kaplan** (1959-) res. Cape Coral, FL

        5 **Bonnie (Callan) Kaplan** (1963-) m. ? Ruppert, div, m. John Reinke res. Cape Coral. FL

          6 **Sean Ruppert** (1983-) m. Carolyn Petrucelli, res. Pittsburgh, PA

            7 **Son** ?

          6 **Scott** (1991?-)

ISRAEL KAPLAN

1 **Himan Kaplan** b. Grodno, Belarus m. Eavie Appelbaum res. Grodno, Belarus

    2 **Isaac Kaplan** (ca. 1861-1931) m.?, res. Grodno, Belarus, Chomsk, Belarus, Brooklyn, NY

        3 **Israel (Yisroel) Kaplan** (ca. 1878-1970) m. Mollie (Malka) (ca. 1881-?), res. Grodno, Belarus, New York, NY, Ellenville, NY, Brooklyn, NY

            4 **Louis Kaplan** (1904-?) m. Matilda (Maddie), Brooklyn, NY

            4 **Abraham Kaplan** (1906-?)

            4 **Ella Kaplan** (1908-?)

            4 **Sarah Kaplan** (1913-?) m. Charles Levy

SAMUEL KAPLAN

1 **Himan Kaplan** b. Grodno, Belarus m. Eavie Appelbaum, res. Grodno, Belarus

    2 **Isaac Kaplan** (ca. 1861-1931) m.?, res. Grodno, Belarus, Chomsk, Belarus, Brooklyn, NY

        3 **Samuel (Shmulkeh) Kaplan** (ca. 1895-?) m. Dora div., res. Grodno, Belarus, Brooklyn, NY

       ★2nd wife of **Samuel Kaplan** m. Ida

            4 Son

            4 Daughter

Rafael Folik HaLevy Muzykant Family Tree

1 **Rafael "Folik" HaLevy Muzykant** d: Bef. 1860

  2 **Leib Baer Muzykant** b: Bef. 1840 in Tarashcha, Kiev, Ukraine d: Bef. 1906 in Europe

    3 **Philip (Rafael HaLevy) Morrison [Muzykant]** b: Abt. 1860 in "Russia" d: Bef. 1942 in Philadelphia, Philadelphia, PA
    +Feiga's Sister Kaplan d: Bef. 1891

      4 **Lipka Morrison [Muzykant]** b: Abt. 1884 in Tarashcha, Kiev, Ukraine d: Bef. 1955 in Philadelphia, PA
      +Max (Michael) Tonick [Titunik] b: 01 May 1882 in Tarashcha, Kiev, Ukraine d: Bef. 1959 in Philadelphia, PA m: Abt. 1907

        5 **Celia Tonick [Titunik]** b: 08 Sep 1908 in Tarashcha, Kiev, Ukraine d: Jul 1984 in Philadelphia, PA
        +William Rudney b: 10 Dec 1904 d: Nov 1977 in Philadelphia, PA m: Aft. 1929

          6 **Phyllis A. Rudney** b: 13 Jun 1933 in Philadelphia, PA
          +David S. Elfont b: 05 May 1929 in Philadelphia, PA d: 06 Sep 1999 in Philadelphia, PA

            7 **Lynne M. Elfont** b: 05 Jul 1955 in Phila., PA

            7 **Arthur B. Elfont** b: 19 Sep 1959 in Phila, PA
            +Ariene H. Zahustecher b: Mar 1957

              8 **Melissa Elfont**

              8 **Alex Elfont**

            7 **Mitchell D. Elfont** b: 19 Sep 1959 in Phila., PA
            +Judith Corey Engelberg b: 15 Mar 1963 in Brooklyn, NY m: 12 Jul 1992 in North Miami, Florida

              8 **Stephanie Elfont** b: 18 Aug 1994 in Plantation, Florida

              8 **Benjamin Elfont** b: 21 Mar 1997 in Plantation, Florida

          6 **Melvin Roy Rudney** b: 23 Apr 1935 in Philadelphia, PA d: Apr 1966
          +ExWife

      4 **Lena Morrison [Muzykant]** b: Abt. 1890 in Tarashcha, Kiev, Ukraine d: Bef. 1942 in Philadelphia, PA
      +Philip Shapiro b: Abt. 1885 d: Bef. 1943 in Philadelphia, PA m: Abt. 1913

5 **Joseph Shapiro** b: Abt. 1915 in Philadelphia, PA
+Pauline b: May 1919 d: Abt. 1985

 6 **Eileen Shapiro** b: 26 Jan 1942
 +Weingrad
 *2nd Husband of Eileen Shapiro:
 +Another Husband

 6 **Philip Shapiro** b: 23 Sep 1946
 +Susan Munz Cohn b: 1952

5 **Jack Shapiro** b: 22 Feb 1919 in Philadelphia, PA d: 28
Feb 1993 in Fort Lauderdale, Florida
+Shirley Bransky b: 01 Feb 1923 in Philadelphia, PA
m: 1943 in Philadelphia, PA

 6 **Larry L. Shapiro** b: 07 May 1947 in Phila., PA
 +Shelly Blackman b: 03 Feb 1950

  7 **Stuart L. Shapiro** b: 01 Dec 1977 in Phila., PA

  7 **Jared A. Shapiro** b: 23 Oct 1980 in Phila., PA

 *2nd Wife of **Larry L. Shapiro**:
 +Mema Joy Kirschenbaum b: 09 Jul 1947
 m: 18 Feb 1997 in Broward Cty, Florida

 6 **Phyllis Shapiro** b: 17 Sep 1955 in Philadelphia, PA
 +Allen M. Rosenzweig b: 20 Jan 1956

  7 **Danielle N. Rosenzweig** b: 02 Oct 1982 in
  Margate, New Jersey

  7 **Lindsay Paige Rosenzweig** b: Abt. 1986 in
  Margate, New Jersey

4 **Fannie Morrison [Muzykant]** b: Abt. 1891 in Tarashcha,
Kiev, Ukraine d: 26 Jan 1971 in Philadelphia, PA
+Sam Dubin b: 1895 in Russia d: 09 Oct 1952 in Phila., PA

 5 **Jack Dubin** b: 20 May 1917 in Philadelphia, PA
 +Miriam B. b: Nov 1921

  6 **Ronald P. Dubin** b: 11 Aug 1947
  +Gail D. b: 16 Feb 1953

   7 **Howard Dubin** b: 1976

   7 **Dana Dubin**

 5 **Sol Dubin** b: 08 Dec 1928 in Philadelphia, PA
 d: 15 Aug 2006 in Moorestown, NJ
 +ExWife

*2nd Wife of **Philip (Rafael HaLevy) Morrison [Muzykant]**:
+Fanny Fagie Kaplan b: Abt. 1870 in "Russia" d: Aft. 1959 in
Philadelphia, PA m: Abt. 1891 in "Russia"

4 **Becky Morrison [Muzykant]** b: 17 Mar 1891 in Tarashcha, Kiev, Ukraine d: 29 Apr 1982 in Philadelphia, PA
+David Weiss b: Abt. 1886 in Russia d: 29 Nov 1949 m: Aft. 1915

>5 **Dorothy Weiss** b: 25 Mar 1927 in Philadelphia, PA
+Joseph J. Weiss b: 02 Nov 1925 in Philadelphia, PA m: 17 Jun 1950 in Philadelphia, PA

>>6 **Deborah Weiss** b: 30 Oct 1952 in Philadelphia, PA
+Mark Sheldon Alper b: 19 Feb 1953

>>>7 **Seth Michael Alper** b: 10 May 1980 in Philadelphia, PA
+Nancy Gabay b: in New York

>>>7 **Rebecca Leigh Alper** b: 27 Feb 1986 in Philadelphia, PA

>>>7 **William Jonathan Alper** b: 1987 in Philadelphia, PA

>>6 **Alan Lester Weiss** b: 26 Nov 1954 in Phila., PA
+Cynthia Lynn Scarlett b: 13 Jan 1965 m: 24 Jun 1988 in Palm Beach Cty, Florida

>>>7 **Brittany Morgan Weiss** b: 1988 in West Palm Beach, FL

>>>7 **Zachary David Weiss** b: 1993 in West Palm Beach, FL

>>>7 **Mason Vaughn Weiss** b: 1995 in West Palm Beach, FL

>>6 **Randall (Rafael) Mark Weiss** b: 14 May 1962 in Philadelphia, PA

>>6 **Amy Rochelle Weiss** b: 17 Aug 1963 in Phila., PA

4 **Anna Morrison [Muzykant]** b: Abt. 1895 in Tarashcha, Kiev, Ukraine d: Bef. 1987
+Morris Zappan b: 14 Apr 1894 in Russia d: Sep 1987 in Philadelphia, PA

>5 **Jack Zappan** b: 14 Jun 1921 in Philadelphia, PA d: 26 Nov 1996 in Philadelphia, PA
+Freda J. b: 14 Jun 1921 m: Abt. 1950

>>6 **Frederick M. Zappan** b: 15 Jul 1952
+SandraM. b: 27 Sep 1953

>>>7 **Jason Zappan** b: 1978

>>>7 **Rory M. Zappan** b: 1982

>>6 **Arlene R. Zappan** b: 19 Nov 1955
+Owen Steven Zibrak b: 09 Apr 1952 Divorce: 2006

7 **Ban Zibrak** b: 09 Oct 1982

7 **Sydney A. Zibrak** b: 15 Jun 1984

5 **Robert Zappan** b: 24 Dec 1924 in Philadelphia, PA
d: 11 May 2004 in Philadelphia, PA
+Jeanette B. b: 25 Mar 1927

6 **Ronald B. Zappan** b: 30 Jul 1948
+Joan B. b:1943

7 **Adam G. Zappan** b: 02 Jul 1972
+Deguang Pan

8 **Nicholas Zappan**

8 **Matthew Zappan**

7 **Jamie L. Zappan** b: Abt. 1979
+Jared Malsom b: Sep 1973

6 **Bruce Zappan** b: 04 Aug 1951
+Merle Joyce Shuman b: 06 May 1953

7 **Justin Zappan**

7 **Melissa Zappan**

4 **Jacob Morrison [Muzykant]** b: 17 Mar 1896 in Tarashcha,
Kiev, Ukraine d: 24 Oct 1980 in Philadelphia, PA
+Sarah (Sara Ryfka) Sears b: 21 Dec 1895 in Poland d: 13 Jun
1988 in Plymouth Meeting, PA

5 **Herman Morrison** b: 06 Dec 1918 in Philadelphia, PA
d: 17 Mar 2007 in Plymouth Meeting, PA
+lda Hoffman b: 23 Feb 1921 in Russia d: 12 Nov 2004 in
Plymouth Meeting, PA m: 1943 in Philadelphia, PA

6 **Denise B. Morrison** b: 1950
+Howard B. Stredler b: 1948

7 **Jennifer I. Stredler** b: 1980

7 **Ian R. Stredler** b: Abt. 1983

6 **Michael Morrison** b: Abt. 1953
+Eva Lynn Milestone b: Sep 1955 m: in Fla

7 **Barri J. Morrison** b: Jan 1982

7 **Zachary Morrison** b: Abt. 1984

7 **Benjamin A. Morrison** b: Abt. 1987

5 **Lillian H. Morrison** b: Dec 1923 in Philadelphia, PA
+Edward H. Goldberg b: 04 May 1922 d: 16 Feb 1988 in
Plymouth Meeting, Pennsylvania

6 **Ronald Goldberg**

6 **Arlene Goldberg**

6 **Cindy Goldberg**

5 **Leonard B. Morrison** b: 14 Feb 1930 in Philadelphia, PA d: 27 Apr 2003 in Garden Grove, California
+Barabara V.

3 **Morris (Moshe) Morrison [Muzykant]** b: Abt. 1870 in Tarashcha, Kiev, Ukraine d: 05 Dec 1943 in Philadelphia, PA
+Fanny (Fajga bat Yakov) b: Abt. 1882 in Kiev, Ukraine d: 20 Jan 1950 in Philadelphia, PA m: Abt. 1900

4 **Elizabeth Morrison [Muzykant]** b: 22 Aug 1903 in Tarashcha, Kiev, Ukraine d: 16 Jan 1991 in Philadelphia, PA
+Reyner

*2nd Husband of **Elizabeth Morrison [Muzykant]**:
+Harry Goldfarb b: 15 Apr 1907 d: 20 Mar 1994 in Philadelphia, PA

4 **Irving (Israel) Morrison [Muzykant]** b: Abt. 1904 in Tarashcha, Kiev, Ukraine d: 1936 in Philadelphia, PA
+Francis Lachman b: 15 Aug 1905 in Pennsylvania d: 09 Feb 1988 in Philadelphia, PA m: Abt. 1924

5 **Rosabel S. Morrison** b: 16 Jan 1927 in Chester, PA d: 03 Nov 2000 in Philadelphia, PA
+Aaron Sklar b: 27 Jul 1925 in Philadelphia, PA d: 1956 in Philadelphia, PA.

6 **Irwin R. Sklar** b: 06 Mar 1952 in Philadelphia, PA
+Phyllis Susan Taransky b: 14 Jan 1956 in Philadelphia, PA m: Jun 1976 in Philadelphia, PA

7 **Adam Eric Sklar** b: Jun 1982 in Phila., PA

6 **Stephen J. Sklar** b: 06 Mar 1952 in Phila., PA
+Marcia H. Cohen b: 17 Apr 1955 in Philadelphia, PA m: Nov 1976 in Yeadon, PA

7 **David Sklar** b: 01 Aug 1983 in Indianapolis, IN

7 **Lisa Sklar** b: Jun 1988 in Indianapolis, IN

*2nd Husband of **Rosabel S. Morrison**:
+Gerald P. Hurst b: 18 Mar 1935

5 **Eileen E, Morrison** b: 16 Dec 1933 in Pennsylvania
+Robert Friedenberg b: 29 Sep 1935

6 **Debra Ellen Friedenberg** b: 10 Jan 1960
+Mame Lawrence Coggan b: 02 Nov 1953

6 **Beth Ann Friedenberg** b: 20 Jul 1962
+Donald W. Plumley b: 04 May 1962

7 **Curtis Jackson Plumley** b: 05 Jun 1990 in Orange Cty, California

7 **Lauren Michiko Plumley** b: 17 Feb 1993 in Orange Cty, California

*2nd Husband of **Eileen E. Morrison**:
+Kenneth G. Oleyar b: 23 Mar 1942

4 **Abe Morrison [Muzykant]** b: Abt. 1906 in Tarashcha, Kiev, Ukraine d: in Black sheep... +Deserted Wife

4 **Louis B. Morrison [Muzykant]** b: 16 Aug 1908 in Tarashcha, Kiev, Ukraine d: 23 Sep 1990 in Philadelphia, PA.
+Millie b: 09 Jun 1906 d: 01 Mar 1976 in Philadelphia, PA

  5 **Charlotte Morrison** b: 01 May 1931 d: Mar 1987 in Canoga Park, Los Angeles, California
  +David Myers

    6 **Vicki Myers** b: Abt. 1950
    +Adams

      7 **Justin Adams**

    *2nd Husband of **Vicki Myers**:
    +Slovick

    6 **Cheryl "Jennifer" Myers** b: Bef. 1955
    +First Husband

    *2nd Husband of **Cheryl "Jennifer" Myers**:
    +Second Husband

    *3rd Husband of **Cheryl "Jennifer" Myers**:
    +Third Husband m: in Atlanta, Fulton, Georgia

*2nd Wife of **Louis B. Morrison [Muzykant]**:
+Carmella V. Martini b: 07 Feb 1921 m: 1959

4 **Sadie (Sonja) Morrison [Muzykant]** b: 05 Dec 1911 in Tarashcha, Kiev, Ukraine d: 10 Mar 1986 in Philadelphia, PA
+Israel Kelner b: 26 Jul 1906 in Russia d: 28 Dec 1965 in Philadelphia, PA

  5 **Doris Kelner** b: 03 Feb 1930 in Philadelphia, PA
  +Morton Goodman b: 18 Oct 1916

    6 **Robert Bruce Goodman** b: 07 May 1958 in Philadelphia, PA d: Abt. 1993

    6 **Kevin Michael Goodman** b: 31 Mar 1962 in Philadelphia, PA
    +Valerie

      7 **Sharon Goodman** b: 26 Oct 1981 in Philadelphia, PA
      +Brian McNulty

        8 **Brian McNulty, Jr** b: Jan 2004

        8 **Twin McNulty**

        8 **Twin McNulty**

5 **Marlene I. Kelner** b: 28 Oct 1933 in Philadelphia, PA
+First Husband

*2nd Husband of **Marlene I. Kelner:**
+Paul L. Guida b: 23 Sep 1934 in Philadelphia, PA

> 6 **Mindy J. Guida** b: 01 May 1961 in Philadelphia, PA
> +Francis Graham

> > 7 **Kelly Guida** b: 27 Mar 1985 in Phila., PA

> 6 **Perry N. Guida** b: 14 Sep 1964 in Philadelphia, PA
> +Justin's Mother m: Bef. 1983

> > 7 **Justin Guida** b: 1983 in Philadelphia, PA

> *Partner of **Perry N. Guida:**
> +Starr Hall Atiyeh b: 22 Oct 1973 in Los Angeles
> City, California m: Aft. 1983

> > 7 **Savannah Starr Guida** b: 26 Mar 1993 in
> > Los Angeles Cty, California

*3rd Husband of **Marlene I. Kelner:**
+William Stotts m: Jul 1989 in Philadelphia, PA

4 **Hilda Morrison** b: 15 Feb 1915 in Philadelphia, PA
+Norman Goldfarb b: 01 Apr 1914 in Odessa, Russia d: Abt.
1956 in Philadelphia, PA

> 5 **Sheldon Irwin "Sonny" Goldfarb** b: 18 Apr 1941 in
> Philadelphia, PA
> +Harriet Siegel b: Jun 1942 in Baltimore, Maryland m:
> 1966 in Baltimore, Maryland

> > 6 **Debra llene (Davida Yocheved) Goldfarb** b: 16 Jan
> > 1967 in Baltimore, Maryland
> > +Gregory Stevens b: 28 Dec 1960

> > > 7 **Mandi Beth (Basa Malka) Stevens** b: 12 Feb
> > > 1993 in Baltimore, Maryland

> > > 7 **Emily Jayne (Chana Leah) Stevens** b: 13 Aug
> > > 1998 in Baltimore, Maryland

> *2nd Wife of **Sheldon Irwin "Sonny" Goldfarb:**
> +Nina m: Bef. 1984

> *3rd Wife of **Sheldon Irwin "Sonny" Goldfarb:**
> +Lorriane Louise Decrescenzo b: 31 May 1938 in
> Brooklyn, NY m: 31 Mar 1985 in Broward Cty, FL

> *4th Wife of **Sheldon Irwin "Sonny" Goldfarb:**
> +Gayle Eiris Levitan b: 22 Aug 1947 in Larchmont, NY
> m: 12 Dec 2001 in Broward Cty, FL

> 5 **Marshall Ronald "Buddy" Goldfarb** b: 27 Feb
> 1945 in Philadelphia, PA
> +Pauline Brown m: Bef. 1988

*2nd Wife of **Marshall Ronald "Buddy" Goldfarb**:
+Clara Ann Seay Daniels b: 21 Dec 1942 in Burleson Cty, TX m: 29 Feb 1988 in Travis Cty, TX. Divorce: Aft. 1988

4 **Joseph Morrison** b: 04 Aug 1917 in Philadelphia, PA d: 28 Dec 2003 in O'Fallon, Saint Charles, Missouri
+Ruth B. Rossoff b: 05 May 1921 in Philadelphia, PA d: 23 Feb 1999 in Phoenix, Maricopa, Arizona

> 5 **Mona S. Morrison** b: 19 May 1947 in Philadelphia, PA
> +David Glucksman

> *2nd Husband of **Mona S. Morrison**:
> +Michael I. Santow b: 07 Sep 1944 Divorce: Bef. 2006

> 5 **Ellen Joy Morrison** b: 06 Oct 1949 in Philadelphia, PA
> +Howard Bobb b: Abt. 1949 Divorce: Bef. 1992

>> 6 **Meredith Stacey Bobb** b: 20 Nov 1974 in Abington, PA

>> 6 **Devon Eric Bobb** b: 18 Aug 1978 in Abington, PA

*2nd Husband of **Ellen Joy Morrison**:
+Michael Doheny b: 22 Feb 1953 in Abington, PA m: 17 Sep 2005 in Conshohocken, PA

> 5 **Terri Rae Morrison** b: 28 Jun 1955 in Philadelphia, PA
> +Billy Lee Marr b: 06 Dec 1948

>> 6 **Colin M. Marr** b: 06 Jul 1980 in Waukesha, WI

>> 6 **Austin Marr** b: 28 Oct 1986 in Phoenix, AZ

4 **Nathan Morrison** b: 20 Mar 1923 in Philadelphia, PA d: 15 Sep 1999 in Gilbertsville, PA
+Henriettta Penny Fine b: Abt. 1924 in Pennsylvania m: 1942

> 5 **Michele L. "Miki" Morrison** b: 08 Aug 1944 in Philadelphia, PA
> +Hany E. Povey b: 30 Jan 1945

>> 6 **Tracey E. Povey** b: 08 Aug 1970 in Phila., PA
>> +Kenin McGovem

>> 6 **Kelly Ann Povey** b: 18 Sep 1974 in Phila., PA
>> +Richard B. Plexico b: 1967

>>> 7 **Alexus Julia Plexico** b: Jan 2003 in Middleton, PA

> 5 **Ronald Dean "Ronnie" Morrison** b: 20 Mar 1948 in Philadelphia, PA
> +Carol Ottaviano Divorce: in aft 1972

>> 6 **Stephen David Morrison** b: 05 Jul 1970 in Philadelphia, PA
>> +Maribeth Kushnerock b: Jun 1970

7 **Grade Marie Morrison** b: 06 Jul 2003 in
Sellersville, PA

7 **Sarah Jane Morrison** b: Sep 2005 in
Sellersville, PA

6 **Ian Charles Morrison** b: 13 Mar 1972 in
Philadelphia, PA

5 **Barry Jay Morrison** b: 23 Mar 1949 in Philadelphia, PA
+Lynne Cuono b: 26 Jun 1952

*2nd Wife of **Nathan Morrison**:
+SecondWife m: Aft. 1949

*3rd Wife of **Nathan Morrison**:
+Lorraine b: 19 Jan 1938 m: Bef. 1999

3 **Tillie (Toba) Muzykant** b: Abt. 1874 in Tarashcha, Kiev, Ukraine
d: 04 Apr 1956 in Brooklyn, Kings, New York
+Yehuda Lib HaKohane d: Bef. 1908

4 **Morris Kaplan** b: 15 Sep 1895 in Kiev, Ukraine d: 20 Apr
1967 in Brooklyn, Kings, New York
+Gertrude (Golda) Rosenthal b: Abt. 1894 in Baltimore,
MD d: 23 Mar 1967 in Brooklyn, NY m: Bef. 1918

5 **Lillian (Liba) Kaplan** b: 04 Apr 1918 in New York, NY
d: 2008
+Samuel Goodman [Guttman] b: 07 Jul 1911 in Mitau,
Latvia d: 27 Mar 2001 in Livingston, NJ m: 19 Oct 1938
in New York, NY

6 **Paulette Goodman** b: 30 Sep 1940 in Brooklyn, NY
+Saul Norman (Shlomo Natan) Weinstein
b: 06 Jul 1937 in Brooklyn, NY m: 25 Jan 1959 in
Brooklyn, NY Divorce: 1971 in NJ

7 **Tori Sue Weinstein** b: 21 Apr 1961 in
Brooklyn, NY

7 **Cindy Ellen Weinstein** b: 06 Jul 1963 in
Brooklyn, NY
+Jeffrey Jay (Yaakov Yosef) Blustein b: 05 Aug
1957 in Brooklyn, NY m: 20 Nov 1988 in
Morristown, NJ Divorce: 11 Mar 2005

8 **Emily Rose (Ema Raizl) Blustein** b: 23
Feb 1992 in Livingston, Essex, NJ

8 **Andrew Jeremy (Mordechai Yirmiyahu)
Blustein** b: 11 Dec 1995 in Livingston, NJ

*2nd Husband of **Paulette Goodman**:
+Jack Bruce Edelson b: 28 Oct 1938 in New York, NY
d: 30 Dec 2004 in Denville, NJ m: 20 May 1973 in
New York, NY

      6 **Michael Goodman** b: 17 Jun 1944 in Brooklyn, NY
      +Rita S. Zeiger b: 19 Nov 1947 m: 10 Mar 1968 in
      Brooklyn, NY

          7 **Lisa (Leah) Ellen Goodman** b: 12 Aug 1980
          in Brooklyn, NY

    5 **Joseph Kaplan** b: 31 Jan 1920 in New York, NY
    d: 23 Sep 1984 in Brooklyn, NY
    +Ethel Maldauer m: 05 Mar 1955 Divorce: Aft. 1959

      6 **Terry B. Kaplan** b: 14 Nov 1956 in Brooklyn, NY
      +Martha Farfan b: 15 Sep 1955

      *2nd Wife of **Terry B. Kaplan**:
      +Constanza Melo b: May 1961

      6 **Harvey Benjamin Kaplan** b: 02 Jun 1959 in
      Brooklyn, NY
      +Janet

*2nd Husband of **Tillie (Toba) Muzykant**:
+Isaac Kaplan b: Abt. 1870 in Chomsk, Belarus d: 05 Oct 1931 in
New York m: 1908 in USA

    4 **Anna Kaplan** b: 05 Jul 1913 in Brooklyn, NY d: 2012
    +Louis Levitt b: 02 Jul 1911 in Brooklyn, NY d: 06 Jun 1978
    in Brooklyn, NY m: 12 Jan 1947 in Brooklyn, NY

      5 **Ira Stephen Levitt** b: 02 Feb 1948 in Brooklyn, NY
      +Barbara A. Harfosh b: 30 Jan 1950 m: 14 Aug 1977

        6 **Joshua Michael Levitt** b: 27 Jun 1986

      5 **Joel Stanley Levitt** b: 11 Feb 1949 in Brooklyn, NY
      +Barbara L. Robinson b: 04 Oct 1950 in Brooklyn, NY
      m: 08 Apr 1973 in Laurelton, NY

        6 **Lia Jill Levitt** b: 08 Mar 1980 in Danbury, CT

        6 **Jessica Taryn Levitt** b: 26 May 1983 in Danbury, CT

          7 **Haley Shianne Bittner**, (2011-) res. New
          Milford, CT

          7 **Briella Kylee Bittner**, (2011-), res.
          New Milford, CT

          7 **Joseph (Joey) Ashton Bittner**, (2016-), res.
          New Milford, CT

3 **Liba Muzykant** b: in Tarasheha, Kiev, Ukraine
d: in Philadelphia, PA
+Husband

    4 **Moshe "Muzzy"**

    4 **Anna**

    4 **Mitzi**

3 **Female Muzykant** b: in Tarashcha, Kiev, Ukraine
2 **Male Muzykant** b: Aft. 1840
  3 **Rafael Musikant** b: 1866 in Tarashcha, Kiev, Ukraine
  +Tauba Fotmann b: 1881 in Tarashcha, Ukraine
    4 **Moses Musikant** b: 1897 in Tarashcha, Kiev, Ukraine

Liba Muzykant Family Tree

Generation 1

1. **Liba Musicant**-1 was born about 1868 in Tarashcha, Kyiv, Ukraine. Midwife in Russia. Immigrated to USA 1914.
• Yosef Monastersky son of Okiva Monastersky and Naomi ?.
• Yosef Monastersky and **Liba Musicant** married. They had the following children:

    2. i. **Anna "Nachomi" Monastersky** was born on 25 May 1898 in Tarashcha, Kyiv, Ukraine. She died on 06 Mar 1990 in Philadelphia, Pennsylvania, USA.

    3. ii. **Minnie Monastersky** was bom on 08 Jun 1901 in Russia. She married Morris Merlin in 1915 in Philadelphia, Pennsylvania, USA. She died on 14 Feb 1987 in Lafayette Hill, Philadelphia, Pennsylvania.

    4. iii. **Morris (Moshe) "Muzzy" Abbott** was bom on 24 Mar 1898 in Tarashcha, Kyiv, Ukraine. He married Yetta Masbitz after 1951. He died in Aug 1983 in Philadelphia, Pennsylvania, USA.

    5. iv. **Yaacov "Yasha" Monastersky** was born in 1897 in Tarashcha, Kyiv, Ukraine. He died in 1933 in Russia.

• Morris April.
• Morris April and **Liba Musicant** married. They had no children.

Generation 2

2. **Anna "Nachomi" Monastersky**-2 (Liba-1) was born on 25 May 1898 in Tarashcha, Kyiv, Ukraine. She died on 06 Mar 1990 in Philadelphia, Pennsylvania, USA. Named changed from Monastersky to Abbott when parents emigrated to USA. Known as Tante Chemal
• Louis Fraiden (Freed) was born on 10 Nov 1898 in Kiev, Kyiv, Ukraine. He died on 27 Oct 1962 in Philadelphia, Pennsylvania, USA.
• Louis Fraiden (Freed) and **Anna "Nachomi" Monastersky** married. They had the following children:

    6. i. **Joseph L. Freed** was born on 16 Feb 1919 in Philadelphia, PA. He married Mollie Benen in 1942 in Philadelphia, PA. He died on 23 Mar 1992 in Philadelphia, Pennsylvania, USA.

    7. ii. **Harold "Hershel" B. Freed** was born on 13 Nov 1920. He died before 2010.

    8. iii. **Jeanette Freed** was born on 17 Oct 1929 in Philadelphia, PA. She married Phil Shoap on 05 Jun 1949 in Philadelphia, PA.

    9. iv. **Dolly Freed** was born on 17 Oct 1929 in Philadelphia, Pennsylvania, USA. She married Steve Kriesman in 1948. She died on 07 Apr 2017 in Philadelphia, PA.

3. Minnie Monastersky-2 (Liba-1) was born on 08 Jun 1901 in Russia. She died on 14 Feb 1987 in Lafayette Hill, Philadelphia, Pennsylvania. DOB actually June 8, 1894? Or given as such to get SS benefits? ss 171-05-0501. Hebrew Name Chana Mirka
• Morris Merlin son of Chaim Gedalia Merlinski and Chana Leah Hochberg was born on 03 Jan 1890 in Gaysin, Vinnytsya, Ukraine. He died on 08 Dec 1935 in Philadelphia, PA. Sponsor was brother Merlinsky (1922 S 5th St. Philadelphia). Hebrew Name Moshe Shmuel, Born Moses Merlinsky. Barber. Had children with another woman in Russia or Argentina. Have a 5 million mark bill from Germany (worthless now). He had a lot of $$ in Germany. Birth place possibly Terelitza, Russia
• Morris Merlin and **Minnie Monastersky** were married in 1915 in Philadelphia, PA. They had the following children:

> 10. i. **Joseph Merlin** was born on 08 Jun 1917 in Philadelphia, PA. He married Sara Unis on 11 Sep 1938 in Philadelphia, PA. He died on 21 Apr 2008 in Philadelphia, PA.

> 11. ii. **Evelyn Merlin** was born on 15 Apr 1919 in Philadelphia, PA. She married Pinya Yonkovitz on 14 Nov 1937 in Philadelphia, PA. She died on 21 Feb 1981 in Philadelphia, PA.

> 12. iii. **Sue (Sylvia) Merlin** was born on 15 Apr 1919 in Philadelphia, Pennsylvania, USA. She married Harold Theodore Rappoport on 22 Jan 1939 in Philadelphia, PA. She died on 16 Nov 1957 in Philadelphia, Pennsylvania, USA.

> 13. iv. **Daris Merlin** was born on 26 Mar 1930 in Philadelphia, PA. She married Irvin Robert Kanas on 27 Jun 1948 in Philadelphia, PA. She died on 27 Dec 2016 in Middle, Cape May, New Jersey, USA.

• Morris Feldman. He died on 24 Dec 1972.
• Morris Feldman and **Minnie Monastersky** married. They had no children.

4. Morris (Moshe) "Muzzy" Abbott-2 (Liba-1) was born on 24 Mar 1898 in Tarashcha, Kyiv, Ukraine. He died in Aug 1983 in Philadelphia, Pennsylvania, USA. Changed his name to Abbott after the word Monastery.
• Yetta Masbitz. She died on 21 Aug 1991.
• Morris (Moshe) "Muzzy" Abbott and Yetta Masbitz were married after 1951. They had no children.
• Etta Rosenblum. She died before 1983.
• Morris (Moshe) "Muzzy" Abbott and Etta Rosenblum were married in 1921 in Philadelphia, Pennsylvania, USA. They had the following children:

> 14. i. **Joseph Abbott.**

5. **Yaacov "Yasha" Monastersky**-2 (Liba-1) was born in 1897 in Tarashcha, Kyiv, Ukraine. He died in 1933 in Russia. Sent to Siberia, children were in Heber, Israel.
• Faga ?.
• **Yaacov "Yasha" Monastersky** and Faga ? married. They had the following children:

> 15. i. **Yossel Monastersky**.
>
> ii. ? **Monastersky**.
>
> iii. ? **Monastersky**.
>
> iv. ? **Monastersky**.

Generation 3

6. **Joseph L. Freed**-3 (Anna "Nachomi"-2, Liba-1) was born on 16 Feb 1919 in Philadelphia, PA. He died on 23 Mar 1992 in Philadelphia, PA.
• Mollie Benen was born on 25 Nov 1922. She died on 21 Jul 2006 in Philadelphia, PA.
• **Joseph L. Freed** and Mollie Benen were married in 1942 in Philadelphia, Pennsylvania, USA. They had the following children:

> 16. i. **Belle Sharon Freed** was born on 27 Jan 1947 in Philadelphia, Pennsylvania, USA.
>
> 17. ii. **Arthur Freed** was born on 14 Mar 1951 in Philadelphia, Pennsylvania, USA.

7. **Harold "Hershel" B. Freed**-3 (Anna "Nachomi"-2, Liba-1) was born on 13 Nov 1920. He died before 2010.
• Naomi Heilveil was born on 02 Nov 1919. She died on 14 Jun 1994.
• **Harold "Hershel" B. Freed** and Naomi Heilveil married. They had the following children:

> 18. i. **Richard U. Freed** was born on 27 Apr 1949 in Philadelphia, PA.
>
> 19. ii. **Sidney B. Freed** was born on 08 Feb 1951.
>
> 20. iii. **Lawrence Freed** was born on 17 Mar 1958 in Philadelphia, PA. He married Sherre Pendergast Fish on 21 Apr 1985.

8. **Jeanette Freed**-3 (Anna "Nachomi"-2, Liba-1) was born on 17 Oct 1929 in Philadelphia, PA.
• Phil Shoap was bom on 07 Jan 1924 in Philadelphia, Pennsylvania, USA.
• Phil Shoap and **Jeanette Freed** were married on 05 Jun 1949 in Philadelphia, Pennsylvania, USA. They had the following children:

> 21. i. **Allan Shoap** was born on 27 Feb 1951 in Philadelphia, PA.
>
> 22. ii. **Linda Shoap** was born on 16 Dec 1954.

9.   **Dolly Freed**-3 (Anna "Nachomi"-2, Liba-1) was born on 17 Oct 1929 in Philadelphia, PA. She died on 07 Apr 2017 in Philadelphia, PA.
• Steve Kriesman was born on 03 Nov 1928.
• Steve Kriesman and Dolly Freed were married in 1948. They had the following children:

> 23. i. **Gwenn Kriesman** was born on 14 Jun 1950 in Philadelphia, PA.

• Daniel Marable was born on 09 Sep 1925. He died on 06 Apr 2000 in Levittown, Bucks, Pennsylvania, USA.
• Daniel Marable and **Dolly Freed** were married on 04 Aug 1985. They had the following children:

> i.   **Donato Marable**.

10.   **Joseph Merlin**-3 (Minnie-2, Liba-1) was born on 08 Jun 1917 in Philadelphia, PA. He died on 21 Apr 2008 in Philadelphia, PA. Butcher
• Sara Unis was born on 16 Nov 1916 in Philadelphia, PA. She died on 10 Sep 2001 in West Palm Beach, FL.
• **Joseph Merlin** and Sara Unis were married on 11 Sep 1938 in Philadelphia, PA. They had the following children:

> 24. i. **Barbara Merlin** was born on 14 Oct 1943 in Philadelphia, PA. She married Allan E. Gomer on 16 Apr 1961 in Philadelphia, PA. She died on 02 Feb 2010 in Philadelphia, PA.

> ii. **Martin Stanley Merlin** was born in 1946. He died in 1963 in Philadelphia, PA. Died at age 19 or 20. Sherly Levin has dob 11-8-1939 and death 2-18-1959

11.   **Evelyn Merlin**-3 (Minnie-2, Liba-1) was born on 15 Apr 1919 in Philadelphia, PA. She died on 21 Feb 1981 in Philadelphia, PA. ss 160-01-2881. Hebrew name Yocheved bat Moshe Shmuel
• Pinya Yonkovitz son of Harry Goldstein (Yonkovitz) and Clara Cotter was born on 03 Nov 1916 in Philadelphia, PA. He died on 05 Oct 1999 in Alexandria, VA.
• Pinya Yonkovitz and **Evelyn Merlin** were married on 14 Nov 1937 in Philadelphia, PA. They had the following children:

> 25. i. **Sandra Yonkovitz** was bom on 11 Oct 1941 in Philadelphia, PA. She married Kenneth Kozlin on 21 Apr 1963 in Philadelphia, PA.

> 26. ii. **Myra Joy Yonkovitz** was bom on 04 Apr 1948 in Philadelphia, PA. She married Steven Lee Silverstein on 30 Dec 1973 in Phila., PA.

12. **Sue (Sylvia) Merlin**-3 (Minnie-2, Liba-1) was born on 15 Apr 1919 in Philadelphia, PA. She died on 16 Nov 1957 in Philadelphia, PA. Hairdresser
• Harold Theodore Rappoport was born on 16 Dec 1915 in Philadelphia, Pennsylvania, USA. He died on 27 Jul 1980 in San Jose, Los Angeles, California, USA.
• Harold Theodore Rappoport and **Sue (Sylvia) Merlin** were married on 22 Jan 1939 in Philadelphia, PA. They had the following children:

> 27. i. **Marvin Stanton Rappoport** was born on 28 Jan 1940 in Philadelphia, PA. He married Adele Goodman on 16 Oct 1960 in Philadelphia, PA. He died on 18 Jul 2015 in Philadelphia, PA.

> 28. ii. **Craig Robert Rappoport** was born on 27 Apr 1954 in Philadelphia, PA. He married Debra Jean Goldberg on 23 Sep 1973.

> 29. iii. **Jeffrey Hugh Rappoport** was born on 10 Mar 1950 in Philadelphia, PA. He married Evie Kusher on 29 May 1972 in Brooklyn, NY.

13. **Daris Merlin**-3 (Minnie-2, Liba-1) was born on 26 Mar 1930 in Philadelphia, PA. She died on 27 Dec 2016 in Middle, Cape May, NJ. Hebrew Name Devorah bat Chana Mirka
• Irvin Robert Kanas was born on 14 Dec 1927. He died on 13 Feb 2011 in Middle, Cape May, NJ.
• Irvin Robert Kanas and **Daris Merlin** were married on 27 Jun 1948 in Philadelphia, PA. They had the following children:

> 30. i. **Merle S Kanas** was born on 29 Mar 1950 in Philadelphia, PA. She married Robert B Puller on 29 Aug 1993.

> 31. ii. **Guy Rory Kanas** was born on 10 Dec 1953.

> iii. **Susan L Kanas** was born on 10 Nov 1959. She married Sam W Gish III on 22 Mar 1987.

14. **Joseph Abbott**-3 (Morris (Moshe) "Muzzy"-2, Liba-1). Died of Lou Gehrig's Disease.
• Leah ?.
• **Joseph Abbott** and Leah ? married. They had the following children:

> i. ? **Abbott**,

> ii. ? **Abbott**,

> iii. ? **Abbott**.

> iv. **Joseph Abbott**.

• ?.

- **Joseph Abbott** and ? married. They had the following children:

    i. ? **Abbott**,

    ii. ? **Abbott**.

    iii. **Joseph Abbott Jr.**

15. **Yossel Monastersky**-3 (Yaacov "Yasha"-2, Liba-1). Moved to Israel after WWII
- Gita ?
- **Yossel Monastersky** and Gita ? married. They had the following children:

    32. i. **Yasha Monastersky**.

    ii. ? **Monastersky**.

    iii. ? **Monastersky**.

Generation 4

16. **Belle Sharon Freed**-4 (Joseph L.-3, Anna "Nachomi"-2, Liba-1) was born on 27 Jan 1947 in Philadelphia, PA.
- Raymond Hirn was born on 22 Apr 1945.
- Raymond Hirn and **Belle Sharon Freed** married. They had the following children:

    i. **Jeffrey Hirn** was born on 23 Nov 1983.

17. **Arthur Freed**-4 (Joseph L.-3, Anna "Nachomi"-2, Liba-1) was bom on 14 Mar 1951 in Philadelphia, PA.
- Carol Borden was born on 16 Apr 1955.
- **Arthur Freed** and Carol Borden married. They had the following children:

    i. **Joseph Borden Freed** was born on 05 Jun 1997 in Baltimore, MD.

18. **Richard U. Freed**-4 (Harold "Hershel" B.-3, Anna "Nachomi"-2, Liba-1) was born on 27 Apr 1949 in Philadelphia, PA.
- Sondra Lee Bogdon was born on 15 Dec 1957.
- Richard U. Freed and Sondra Lee Bogdon married. They had the following children:

    i. **Michael John Freed** was born on 30 Oct 1982.

19. **Sidney B. Freed**-4 (Harold "Hershel" B.-3, Anna "Nachomi"-2, Liba-1) was born on 08 Feb 1951.
- Jody Turner was born on 18 Feb 1957.
- **Sidney B. Freed** and Jody Turner married. They had the following children:

i. **Joshua Lee Freed** was born on 22 Mar 1981.

ii. **Zachary Freed** was born on 09 Feb 1987.

20. **Lawrence Freed**-4 (Harold "Hershel" B.-3, Anna "Nachomi"-2, Liba-1) was born on 17 Mar 1958 in Philadelphia, PA.
• Sherre Pendergast Fish was born on 22 Mar 1961.
• **Lawrence Freed** and Sherre Pendergast Fish were married on 21 Apr 1985. They had the following children:

i. **Brian Gregory Fish** was born on 11 May 1980.

ii. **Nicole Erin Freed** was born on 19 Aug 1986.

iii. **Tiffany Michelle Freed** was born on 12 Feb 1988.

iv. **Shanna Lynn Freed** was born on 16 Mar 1989. 33.

v. **Allie Marie Freed** was born on 02 Jun 1990.

21. **Allan Shoap**-4 (Jeanette-3, Anna "Nachomi"-2, Liba-1) was born on 27 Feb 1951 in Philadelphia, PA.
• Carla Shipman was born on 26 Dec 1953.
• **Allan Shoap** and Carla Shipman married. They had the following children:

i. **Miriam Shoap** was born on 10 Apr 1981 in Fairfax, VA. She married Toni Severance in 2009.

ii. **Evin Shoap** was born on 20 Jan 1984.

22. **Linda Shoap**-4 (Jeanette-3, Anna "Nachomi"-2, Liba-1) was born on 16 Dec 1954.
• Scott Thompson was born on 15 Mar 1950.
• Scott Thompson and **Linda Shoap** married. They had the following children:

i. **Shaun Thompson** was born on 05 Jan 1985 in Georgetown, Delaware. He married Mara Hope Weissman on 02 Aug 2009 in Bensalem, PA.

23. **Gwenn Kriesman**-4 (Dolly-3, Anna "Nachomi"-2, Liba-1) was born on 14 Jun 1950 in Philadelphia, PA.
• Allen Bornstein was born on 28 May 1946.
• Allen Bornstein and **Gwenn Kriesman** married. They had the following children:

34. i. **Ashlee Ann Bornstein** was born on 22 Apr 1987 in Phila., PA.

24. **Barbara Merlin**-4 (Joseph-3, Minnie-2, Liba-1) was born on 14 Oct 1943 in Philadelphia, PA. She died on 02 Feb 2010 in Philadelphia, PA.
• Allan E. Gomer was born on 06 May 1939 in Philadelphia, PA. He died on 12 Jan 2009 in Philadelphia, PA.
• Allan E. Gomer and **Barbara Merlin** were married on 16 Apr 1961 in Philadelphia, PA. They had the following children:

> i. **Jamie Elyse Gomer** was born on 15 Apr 1969 in Philadelphia, PA.

> 35. ii. **Mindy S Gomer** was born on 18 Aug 1962.

25. **Sandra Yonkovitz**-4 (Evelyn-3, Minnie-2, Liba-1) was born on 11 Oct 1941 in Philadelphia, PA.
• Kenneth Kozlin was born on 02 Mar 1939 in Westerly, RI.
• Kenneth Kozlin and **Sandra Yonkovitz** were married on 21 Apr 1963 in Philadelphia, PA. They had the following children:

> i. **David Derek Kozlin** was born on 21 Jun 1967 in Westerly, RI. He married Francine Kate Friedman on 27 Jun 2005 in Brooklyn, NY. Hebrew Name Chanan ben Chaim Zydal ha Cohen

> 36. ii. **Ronald Scott Kozlin** was born on 12 Jun 1969 in Westerly, RI. He married Charlotte Ann Lynch on 23 Sep 1995 in Tampa, FL.

26. **Myra Joy Yonkovitz**-4 (Evelyn-3, Minnie-2, Liba-1) was born on 04 Apr 1948 in Philadelphia, PA. Hebrew Name: Masha Yehudas - named for Morris Merlin & Jake Monarstarsky
• Steven Lee Silverstein son of Aaron Silverstein and Rose Devers was bom on 18 Dec 1950 in Philadelphia, Pennsylvania, USA. He died on 22 Apr 2015 in Las Vegas, Clark, Nevada, USA. Hebrew Name: Zeisel Eliezer
• Steven Lee Silverstein and **Myra Joy Yonkovitz** were married on 30 Dec 1973 in Philadelphia, PA. They had the following children:

> 37. i. **Stacy Beth Silverstein** was bom on 31 Oct 1975 in Wilmington, Delaware. She married David Joseph Simon on 16 Mar 2003 in Paradise Valley, Arizona.

> ii. **Jason Eric Silverstein** was bom on 01 Nov 1982 in Philadelphia, PA. Hebrew Name: Yaacov Tzvi (Hirsch) named for Evelyn Merlin & Harry Goldstein (Yonkovitz).

> iii. **Adam Michael Silverstein** was born on 03 Nov 1985 in Mesa, Maricopa, Arizona, USA. He married David Lindsay on 22 Nov 2013 in California, USA. Hebrew Name: Elijah Tzvi after Lena Gold and William Devers.

27. **Marvin Stanton Rappoport**-4 (Sue (Sylvia)-3, Minnie-2, Liba-1) was born on 28 Jan 1940 in Philadelphia, PA. He died on 18 Jul 2015 in Philadelphia, PA.
• Adele Goodman was born on 15 Feb 1942.
• **Marvin Stanton Rappoport** and Adele Goodman were married on 16 Oct 1960 in Philadelphia, PA. They had the following children:

    38. i. **Jodi Diane Rappoport** was born on 16 Jun 1965 in Philadelphia, PA. She married Robert Palm on 11 Nov 1989.

    39. ii. **Seth Steven Rappoport** was born on 13 Nov 1962 in Elkins Park, PA. He married Francine Weinberg on 20 Oct 1990 in Pennsylvania.

28. **Craig Robert Rappoport**-4 (Sue (Sylvia)-3, Minnie-2, Liba-1) was born on 27 Apr 1954 in Philadelphia, PA.
• Debra Jean Goldberg was born on 23 Jul 1955.
• **Craig Robert Rappoport** and Debra Jean Goldberg were married on 23 Sep 1973. They had the following children:

    40. i. **Shaun M Rappoport** was born on 27 May 1979.

    41. ii. **Joshua Adam Rappoport** was born on 12 Aug 1981.

29. **Jeffrey Hugh Rappoport**-4 (Sue (Sylvia)-3, Minnie-2, Liba-1) was born on 10 Mar 1950 in Philadelphia, PA.
• Evie Kusher was born on 04 Mar 1952.
• **Jeffrey Hugh Rappoport** and Evie Kusher were married on 29 May 1972 in Brooklyn, NY. They had the following children:

    i. **Steven (Shai) Moshe Rappoport** was born on 13 Jan 1978. He married Marissa Scalzo on 09 Nov 2014.

    42. ii. **Talia Riva Rappoport** was born on 02 Jul 1980. She married Yoav Orbach on 29 Aug 2005 in Ramat Razi'el, Jerusalem, Israel.

• Judy Stein was born on 18 Jun 1948.
• **Jeffrey Hugh Rappoport** and Judy Stein were married on 08 May 1988. They had no children.

30. **Merle S Kanas**-4 (Daris-3, Minnie-2, Liba-1) was born on 29 Mar 1950 in Philadelphia, PA.
• Robert B Puller was born on 28 Oct 1958 in Kern, California, USA.
• Robert B Puller and Merle S Kanas were married on 29 Aug 1993. They had the following children:

    i. **Andrew Michael Puller** was born on 26 Jan 1994 in Jewish Autonomous District, Russia Federation. Adopted from Russia in 1994.

31. **Guy Rory Kanas**-4 (Daris-3, Minnie-2, Liba-1) was bom on 10 Dec 1953.
• Gonzala Lopez was born on 10 Jan 1962.
• **Guy Rory Kanas** and Gonzala Lopez married. They had the following children:

>   43. i. **Zina Riva Kanas** was born on 02 May 1982. She married Bryce Harrell on 19 Nov 2008 in Cape May, NJ.

• Sally Prusalitis was born on 05 Jul 1961.
• **Guy Rory Kanas** and Sally Prusalitis were married on 12 Jun 1998. They had no children.

32. **Yasha Monastersky**-4 (Yossel-3, Yaacov "Yasha"-2, Liba-1).
• Yasha Monastersky and unknown spouse married. They had the following children:

>   i. ? **Monastersky**.

>   ii. ? **Monastersky**.

Generation 5

33. **Allie Marie Freed**-5 (Lawrence-4, Harold "Hershel" B.-3, Anna "Nachomi"-2, Liba-1) was born on 02 Jun 1990.
• **Allie Marie Freed** and unknown spouse married. They had the following children:

>   i. **Jordyn Marie ?**.

34. **Ashlee Ann Bornstein**-5 (Gwenn-4, Dolly-3, Anna "Nachomi"-2, Liba-1) was born on 22 Apr 1987 in Philadelphia, PA.
• Matthew L. Check was born about 1974.
• Matthew L. Check and **Ashlee Ann Bornstein** married. They had the following children:

>   i. **Eli Lev Check** was born in 2006 in Abington, Montgomery, PA.

>   ii. **Simon G. Check** was born in 2008 in Abington, Montgomery, PA.

>   iii. **Owen Check**.

35. **Mindy S Gomer**-5 (Barbara-4, Joseph-3, Minnie-2, Liba-1) was born on 18 Aug 1962. name possible spelled Mindee
• Joseph Connell.
• Joseph Connell and **Mindy S Gomer** married. They had no children.

• Ronald N Tolz was born about Apr 1961.
• Ronald N Tolz and **Mindy S Gomer** married. They had the following children:

>   i. **Elanna Lauren Tolz** was born on 14 Mar 1989.

36. **Ronald Scott Kozlin**-5 (Sandra-4, Evelyn-3, Minnie-2, Liba-1) was born on 12 Jun 1969 in Westerly, RI.
• Charlotte Ann Lynch was born on 21 Jun.
• **Ronald Scott Kozlin** and Charlotte Ann Lynch were married on 23 Sep 1995 in Tampa, FL. They had the following children:

> i. **Andrew Davis Kozlin** was born on 04 Jul 1998 in Tampa, FL.

> ii. **Cameron James Kozlin** was born on 30 Jun 2001 in Tampa, FL.

• Lisa Bettencourt was born on 23 Apr 1965 in Massachusetts, USA.
• **Ronald Scott Kozlin** and Lisa Bettencourt were married on 18 Oct 2008 in Dunedin, FL. They had no children.

37. **Stacy Beth Silverstein**-5 (Myra Joy-4, Evelyn-3, Minnie-2, Liba-1) was born on 31 Oct 1975 in Wilmington, Delaware. Hebrew Name Esther Leib named for Louis Silverstein & Esther Blank.
• David Joseph Simon was born on 15 Oct 1968 in Milwaukee, Wisconsin.
• David Joseph Simon and **Stacy Beth Silverstein** were married on 16 Mar 2003 in Paradise Valley, Maricopa, AZ. They had the following children:

> i. **Joshua Daniel Simon** was born on 04 Mar 2008 in Mesa, Maricopa, Arizona, USA. He died on 04 Mar 2008 in Mesa, AZ.

> ii. **Michael Aaron Simon** was born on 15 May 2009 in Mesa, Maricopa, Arizona, USA.Named after Mitzi Merlin and Aaron Silverstein

> iii. **Jacob Ryan Simon** was born on 11 Feb 2012 in Mesa, Maricopa, Arizona, USA. Hebrew Name Yisrael Rachamim (named after Edith Devers Rubin and Ida Simon and Rose Devers Silverstein)

38. **Jodi Diane Rappoport**-5 (Marvin Stanton-4, Sue (Sylvia)-3, Minnie-2, Liba-1) was born on 16 Jun 1965 in Philadelphia, PA.
• Robert Palm was born on 17 Jul 1956. He died on 09 Jan 2001.
• Robert Palm and **Jodi Diane Rappoport** were married on 11 Nov 1989. They had the following children:

> i. **Amanda Brooke Palm** was born on 23 Mar 1991 in Elkins Park, PA.

> ii. **Jordyn Summer Palm** was born on 13 Dec 1993 in Warminster, PA.

39. **Seth Steven Rappoport**-5 (Marvin Stanton-4, Sue (Sylvia)-3, Minnie-2, Liba-1) was born on 13 Nov 1962 in Elkins Park, PA.
• Francine Weinberg was born on 09 Apr 1964.
• **Seth Steven Rappoport** and Francine Weinberg were married on 20 Oct 1990 in Pennsylvania, USA. They had the following children:

> i. **Joshua Ethan Rappoport** was born on 29 Nov 1993 in Manalapan, NJ.

> ii. **Alexis Rappoport** was born on 06 Feb 2000 in Manalapan, NJ.

40. **Shaun M Rappoport**-5 (Craig Robert-4, Sue (Sylvia)-3, Minnie-2, Liba-1) was born on 27 May 1979.
• **Shaun M Rappoport** and unknown spouse married. They had the following children:

    i. **Chace Ryker Rappoport** was born on 07 Nov 2014 in Florida.

41. **Joshua Adam Rappoport**-5 (Craig Robert-4, Sue (Sylvia)-3, Minnie-2, Liba-1) was born on 12 Aug 1981.
• Nichole Lee ? was born on 29 Apr 1983.
• **Joshua Adam Rappoport** and Nichole Lee ? married. They had the following children:

    i. **Brody Rappoport** was born on 03 Aug 2007.

42. **Talia Riva Rappoport**-5 (Jeffrey Hugh-4, Sue (Sylvia)-3, Minnie-2, Liba-1) was born on 02 Jul 1980.
• Yoav Orbach was born on 24 Feb 1981 in Flushing, Queens, NY.
• Yoav Orbach and **Talia Riva Rappoport** were married on 29 Aug 2005 in Ramat Razi'el, Jerusalem, Israel. They had the following children:

    i. **Yakir Elichai Yisrael Orbach** was born on 12 Jul 2008 in Jerusalem.

    ii. **Shoshanah Ayalah Orbach** was born on 09 Aug 2010 in Jerusalem.

    iii. **Amichai Yerucham Orbach** was born on 21 Mar 2013 in Jerusalem.

    iv. **Eliana Chaya Tiferet Orbach** was born on 01 Sep 2015 in Jerusalem.

43. **Zina Riva Kanas**-5 (Guy Rory-4, Daris-3, Minnie-2, Liba-1) was born on 02 May 1982.
• Bryce Harrell was born on 10 Feb 1980.
• Bryce Harrell and **Zina Riva Kanas** were married on 19 Nov 2008 in Cape May, New Jersey, USA. They had the following children:

    i. **Alexander Brandon Harrell** was born on 17 Mar 2010.

Acknowledgements

This family history, a labor of love, could not have been possible without the assistance of the people and resources whose wisdom and generosity are greatly appreciated.

My brother Ira became a major source of memory and memorabilia. He located a treasure trove of Levitt family documents and photographs, forgotten for decades in his basement in Brooklyn. They had been saved by our late aunt Elinor Levitt Axelrod. Our late mother Anna, had also saved a box of Muzykant/Morrison and Kaplan family treasures, which I had shlepped from apartment to apartment and house to house wherever we lived in Brooklyn and Connecticut. The interviews I had done with her in the 1990s, provided a loving and lively account of life in Brooklyn spanning the decades from the turn of the 20th Century to the Sixties.

The exhaustive genealogical research that formed the basis of the Muzykant/Morrison Family Tree was developed by cousin Jeffrey Blustein of New Jersey, who did a remarkable job. Additional and extensive Muzykant family information was generously provided by newly-found cousins Stacy Silverstein Simon of Arizona and Rabbi Jeffrey Rappoport of Jerusalem, on the Apfelbaum side by Dr. Richard Feifer of Connecticut and on the Kaplan side by Joanne Kaplan Handloser of New York.

My wife and partner Barbara, was a constant source of encouragement, amazement and patience (even though I sequestered myself at my desk for countless hours, instead of spending time with my best friend). Still, she is very supportive and proud of this book. Our younger daughter Jessica Bittner, many-a-time saved me from the brink of technological Armageddon, even though I filled her time with my incessant stories of Russian shtetl and Brooklyn shtetl life.

In addition, I'd like to thank and acknowledge the following: The many relatives who were able to fill in the gaps, including my only living aunt, Anne Levitt Kroll and cousins Paul Levitt, Renie Levitt Bailyn, Matthew Levitt, Joshua Levitt, Jacci Davis Rosenthal Schwartz, Gary Levitt, Scott Levitt, Denise Morrison Stredler and the late Herman Morrison, Robert Kaplan, Michael

Kaplan, Richard Kaplan, Deb Kaplan Brindis, Daniel Kaplan, Debbi Bromberg Stanfield, Kenneth Bromberg, Samuel Golden, Eileen Golden Hetson, Joanne Hetson Harrison, Paulette Goodman Edelson, Gary Brownstein and Merle Kanas Pullar.

The family of Victoria Confino Cohen: my friends Stanley Grubman, Vicky Grubman, Denise Grubman Razzagone, the late Celia Grubman and the late Victoria Confino Cohen, herself.

Barbara Siegel Lang, Leah Cohen and the many other Facebook interpreters and commentators from "Tracing the Tribe", "Jewish Genealogy Portal" and "Searching for Kaplan Family".

Friends and relatives of Zachary Solov, including Dean Temple and Zachary's niece Ruthie Rosenfeld McCarthy and the Zachary Solov Foundation, for permission to use photographs from its collection.

Authors utilized in research, including Jane Ziegelman ("97 Orchard: An Edible History of Five Immigrant Families in One New York Tenement"), Murray Friedman ("Philadelphia Jewish Life"), Mark Slobin ("American Klezmer: Its Roots and Offshoots"), Daniel Soyer ("Jewish Immigrant Societies and American Identity in New York, 1880-1939"), Alicia Ault ("Did Ellis Island Officials Really Change the Names of Immigrants?", "Smithsonian Magazine") and Steven J. Zipperstein ("Pogrom: Kishinev and the Tilt of History").

Online resources such as Ancestry.com, FamilySearch.org, MyHeritage.com, JewishGen.org, YivoEncyclopedia.org, History.com, Jewua.org, Berdichev.org, Wikipedia.org and Billboard.com.

Photo sources, including Tenement Museum, Wikimedia Commons, National Portrait Gallery, Centre Pompidou, "New York Daily News", Raleigh Hotel, Thomashefsky Foundation and Erasmus Hall High School.

And a thank you to Lou and Andy Okell at Arkett Publishing, who put my words into print.

I apologize if I have left anyone or anything out or utilized an item without permission. If so, it proves that I am an amateur trying to do my best.

CPSIA information can be obtained
at www.ICGtesting.com
Printed in the USA
BVHW080913100419
545155BV00021B/484/P